Building a Dynamic Europe

This succinct book provides a broad panorama of the key economic policy challenges facing the European Union today. The enlargement of the EU and its lacklustre performance over the last decade in terms of employment and productivity growth have prompted wide-ranging calls for economic reform, both at the EU level and within member states. This volume brings together several leading thinkers in the key areas of policy under discussion, ranging from the institutional design of the enlarged EU for efficient policy-making, to the extent and nature of the integration process in markets such as those of energy and financial services. It includes analyses of the problems of macroeconomic policy co-ordination in the EU and analyses of the reforms in the labour markets and welfare state institutions. Timely and authoritative, this book is accessibly written and will appeal to a wide policy audience.

JORDI GUAL is Professor and Departmental Chair of Economics at IESE Business School (University of Navarra, Barcelona–Madrid). He is editor and co-author of *The Social Dimensions of Employment* (2002), *Europe's Network Industries: Conflicting Priorities. Telecommunications* (1998) and *The Social Challenge of Job Creation: Combating Unemployment in Europe* (1996).

The Public–Private Sector Research Center was created in October 2001. Its mission is to foster co-operation between the private sector and public administrations, as well as the exchange of ideas and initiatives, through dialogue, research and education.

The sponsors of the Center are: Accenture, Barcelona's City Council, BBVA, Diputació de Barcelona, Garrigues Abogados y Asesores Tributarios, the Catalan Government (Generalitat de Catalunya), Merck Sharp & Dohme, the Official Barcelona Chamber of Commerce Industry and Navigation, Patronat Català Pro-Europa, Swiss Life (Spain), Telefónica, S.A. and T-Systems.

IESE Business School — PS-PS

University of Navarra

Building a
Dynamic Europe

The Key Policy Debates

EDITED BY JORDI GUAL

PUBLISHED BY THE PRESS SYNDICATE OF THE UNIVERSITY OF CAMBRIDGE
The Pitt Building, Trumpington Street, Cambridge, United Kingdom

CAMBRIDGE UNIVERSITY PRESS
The Edinburgh Building, Cambridge, CB2 2RU, UK
40 West 20th Street, New York, NY 10011-4211, USA
477 Williamstown Road, Port Melbourne, VIC 3207, Australia
Ruiz de Alarcón 13, 28014 Madrid, Spain
Dock House, The Waterfront, Cape Town 8001, South Africa

http://www.cambridge.org

First published 2004

Printed in the United Kingdom at the University Press, Cambridge

Typeface Sabon 10/13 pt.   *System* LaTeX 2_ε [TB]

A catalogue record for this book is available from the British Library

ISBN 0 521 82734 5 hardback

Contents

Figures

Tables

Contributors

Francesco Giavazzi
Professor of Economics, Vice-rector and Fellow of IGIER
Innocenzo Gasparini Institute for Economic Research,
  Bocconi University, Italy

Jordi Gual
Professor and Chairman of the Economics Department
Academic Director of the Public–Private Sector
  Research Center
IESE Business School
University of Navarra, Barcelona

Assar Lindbeck
Professor of Economics
Institute for International Economic Studies
Stockholm University

David M. Newbery
Professor of Economics
Director, Department of Applied Economics
Cambridge University

Gérard Roland
Professor of Economics
University of California, Berkeley

Acknowledgements

The idea of this book grew out of an international conference on economic reforms in Europe which took place at the IESE Business School in the autumn of 2001, a few months before the Barcelona European Council of 2002. The support provided for that conference by the Fundación Ramón Areces and the Fundación ICO and in particular the impulse provided by Roman Escolano are gratefully acknowledged. Several of the chapters in this book were first presented at that conference and benefited from the contributions of leading experts and practitioners attending the meeting.

I would like to acknowledge also the support of the Public–Private Sector Research Center at the IESE Business School, which has made possible the publication of the revised conference papers, adding contributions with the goal of providing a broad analysis of the key policy debates in the European Union. The support of Jordi Canals, dean of the IESE Business School, has been fundamental for the completion of this project. Teresa Sanjaume and Susana Minguell also provided invaluable support at different stages in the preparation of the conference and the volume.

Introduction

JORDI GUAL

The European Council adopted bold strategic objectives for the economy of the European Union at its summit meeting in Lisbon in 2000. The Council aimed to achieve nothing less than the world's most innovative and dynamic knowledge-based economy within a decade, that is to say by 2010.

The adoption of clear and ambitious objectives made sense to the extent that it gave focus and direction to EU policy-making. Moreover, the authors of the Lisbon agenda were acting on the assumption – appropriate under the circumstances – that the achievement of a dynamic economy was a precondition for the successful carrying-out of the sweeping political transformation of the Union then underway.

This transformation includes the enlargement of the Union from fifteen to up to twenty-seven countries, and the political and institutional reorganization of the Union, including a new constitution that will modify the original founding treaties. This will take place through an intergovernmental conference on the basis of the preparatory work being done by the European Convention on the Future of Europe.

As such, the political landscape of the European Union is on the verge of profound transformation. The result will likely be significant economic change throughout the Union, bringing political conflict among member states in its wake. The opening of the EU to new member states in the East will result, in the short term, in lower per capita income and a higher proportion of the Union's population engaged in agriculture. This development will necessitate a revision of the nature and scale of the two EU policies that consume the largest share of the Union's budget – the common agricultural policy and the regional policy. It will also have far-reaching consequences for income distribution throughout the EU.

Enlargement will also lead to significant EU-wide changes in economic structure, as the new member states begin to compete with

1

existing members and specialization patterns adjust to the new realities. This process, although destined to prove beneficial in the aggregate, will surely lead to increased migration and the prospect of strained social relations in some parts of the Union. As with any process of market integration, the overall benefit runs alongside a non-negligible income redistribution effect, as some social groups gain and others lose from market enlargement.

Similarly, the political reform of the Union – inevitable if the system is to function effectively after absorbing twelve new members – will entail a new distribution of political and economic power as states seek to protect vital economic interests and to enhance their power *vis à vis* other member states in the new political institutions.

Enlargement and the revision of the EU treaties are complex political undertakings that will impose significant economic costs on member states. This is why the implementation of the Lisbon agenda remains an important objective for Europe: members will have an easier time adjusting to the painful political and economic changes that will come in the wake of enlargement if Europe is experiencing rapid and solid economic growth.

A dynamic economy, therefore, must remain a key objective of the European Union's *political* strategy in the years ahead. Europe must aim for and sustain high rates of economic growth – growth based on employment creation and a strong rise in the rate of productivity. Such growth will result in rising per capita income over the long term, which, in turn, will provide Europe with the resources it needs to maintain the social and cohesion policies that enjoy strong support in many European countries, and which European leaders vowed to maintain in the Lisbon declaration.

Over the past ten to fifteen years the EU's economic performance has been less than outstanding. If Europe is to achieve the Lisbon objectives, member states will have no choice but to introduce fundamental economic reforms. It was recognition of this reality that led to the adoption of the Lisbon agenda in the first place.

The purpose of this book is to analyse key policy reforms aimed at bringing about the kind of economic dynamism Europe so sorely needs. Its contributors, drawn from across Europe, pay particular attention to macroeconomic policy management and structural reform.

Francesco Giavazzi (chapter 4) analyses some of the most controversial issues in macroeconomic management in Europe today. He takes a fresh look at the challenges faced by national fiscal authorities when co-ordinating macroeconomic policies within the budgetary constraints imposed by the Growth and Stability Pact (GSP) and by the European Central Bank (ECB). He also explores the ins and outs of European Central Bank governance in an enlarged Europe, and suggests how to properly interpret significant inflation differentials and large current account deficits in the euro zone.

Assar Lindbeck (chapter 2) turns a spotlight on to structural reforms related to labour markets and the functioning of the welfare state. He maintains that significant reforms are needed to guarantee the viability of social welfare programmes, and to bring them into line with changing personal behavioural patterns, new socioeconomic conditions and the exigencies of deepening economic integration throughout the European Union.

Lindbeck's analysis is wide-ranging. It takes the reader on a journey through the human lifespan from cradle to grave, assessing major welfare and employment policies that affect people throughout their lives – child care, employment and income security, health and retirement insurance, and care for the elderly.

David M. Newbery (chapter 3) proposes another set of structural reforms, this time related to the liberalization of markets for network services with a view to creating a unified market throughout the EU. He concentrates on the electricity and gas industries. Newbery maintains that the economics of network industries necessitates a careful balance between regulation and structural change – especially in vertical relationships – if liberalization is to succeed. The opening-up of the network industries market can proceed if due consideration is given to the management of risk and the sustainability of competition within the reformed industry structure.

My contribution to this volume (chapter 5) assesses the policies that have led to the liberalization and integration of financial markets in the European Union. It demonstrates how the EU's approach to the integration of European banking – mutual recognition with a minimal degree of harmonization – differs from other politically less ambitious procedures such as 'national treatment'. By taking a Union-wide approach, the EU has managed to liberalize the banking regulation regime and to avoid undermining those regulations needed to preserve the soundness of the banking industry. Meanwhile, it has achieved a high degree of integration in the sector.

The unifying theme of this volume is that Europe needs to reform its political institutions significantly if it is to meet its objective of greater market integration – the key to a more dynamic European economy. Economic reform in the framework of existing political institutions has run its course.

European economic dynamism and political transformation go hand in hand. A rapidly growing economy will enhance prospects for the transformation of the Union's political institutions by making institutional reform more palatable to national populations. By the same token, the enhancement of the political authority of the EU is vital at a time when the requirements of continued economic integration have outstripped the capacity and willingness of the national states to meet them.

There is widespread agreement in Europe that the current system of institutional decision-making has reached its limit and needs to be drastically overhauled. As Gérard Roland argues in the first chapter of this volume, the current form of governance, whereby the Commission exercises the power of initiative and the Council safeguards the sovereignty of the member states, suffers from a lack of accountability – the well-known democratic deficit. Enlargement is likely to worsen this shortcoming. It comes as no surprise that the Union has not even attempted to apply this approach to decision-making in the spheres of foreign policy, justice and home affairs.

The prevalent alternative form of decision-making until now has been intergovernmental co-ordination. While this approach solves the problem of accountability and safeguards the sovereignty of member states, experience shows that it leaves much to be desired when it comes to the development of new policy initiatives and often leads to outright paralysis. It has been applied – with very limited success – to some of the items on the Lisbon agenda and to issues related to foreign policy and law enforcement, among others.

The deficiencies of current institutional arrangements highlight the need for a new, streamlined approach to decision-making, especially in view of the Union's impending enlargement. Gérard Roland argues that a presidential system made up of a strong executive with a well-defined set of competencies, and subject to the control of the legislature (the European Council), offers the Union the best chance of moving forward with its agenda.

The contributors to this volume present a variety of perspectives on how Europe's current institutional framework tends to impede economic reform. Several of them come to the conclusion that further, meaningful reform cannot take place in the absence of a drastic overhaul of the Union's approach to decision-making. The introduction of the kinds of new institutional arrangements needed to give impetus to economic reform will require a high degree of national, political integration. It is up to the member states to decide whether the gains to be realized from reform and greater economic integration outweigh the cost in terms of foregone national sovereignty. This represents a considerable challenge for the Union, but one it must meet head on. The alternative is getting bogged down in a quagmire of institutional constraints.

The chapters on macroeconomic policy highlight the importance of Europe meeting this challenge. A new political framework enhancing the democratic legitimacy of the European Commission would go a long way toward strengthening the credibility of the Growth and Stability Pact. It would also lead to increased macroeconomic policy co-ordination and improved governance of the European Central Bank.

Concerning welfare reform, measures in this regard are now generally taken outside the Community framework. In practice, the various national states generate welfare reforms based on domestic considerations. A reformed and more accountable European Commission could take the lead in pushing for faster progress in this area. Yet this prospect alarms some member states – the United Kingdom, for example – that wish to continue to treat social and labour policy as domestic matters. Strengthened common political institutions could make the difference. If enlargement leads to a race to the bottom in such areas as social services and corporate tax rates, member states will have to cede some degree of national sovereignty if an effective solution is to be found. The achievement of this objective will require greater legitimacy for Europe's common political institutions.

Much the same is true in regard to the integration of the market for network services. Effective reform will require decisive policies on interconnection, strong measures to maintain a level playing field and strict limits on state aid to national champions in the sector. Again, strong political institutions and a streamlined decision-making process will be crucial.

Integration of the banking sector has been blocked in recent years principally by two factors: (1) interference by member states in cross-border acquisitions and (2) insufficient harmonization. In the absence of further harmonization, the integration of retail markets will be hard to achieve. Doing so may require measures to override national laws, regulations and traditions. On both counts, institutional reforms will be needed to break the deadlock.

The construction of European political institutions has been a long and complex project that will not be accomplished overnight. Europe remains committed to this objective, even more since the collapse of the Berlin Wall. From its inception, the political construction of Europe has been based on economic integration and co-operation, from the establishment of the common market to the introduction of the single currency. Political integration has always lagged far behind. This pattern continues to prevail some fifty years after the signing of the Treaty of Rome.

As things stand now, a strong commitment to co-operation in the matter of economic reform is needed across the continent. This book provides a wealth of ideas on policy changes that can help bring about a more dynamic Europe, the key to which is a vibrant and flourishing economy. Without such an economy, Europe will be hard pressed to meet the political challenges of the twenty-first century.

The contributors to this book make a strong case for the idea that deeper and wider European economic integration requires a dramatic new political impulse in the form of strengthened, common political institutions. The time has come for the European Union's economic integration to advance hand in hand with the continent's political integration.

1 | *The new governance of Europe: parliamentary or presidential?*

GÉRARD ROLAND

Introduction

Research by economists on institutional aspects of the process of European integration has very much focused either on issues of fiscal federalism or on institutions dealing with monetary policy. A huge literature has developed on these issues (see Baldwin and Wyplosz, 2003 forthcoming). This is not surprising since these are areas in which the expertise of economists is quite developed. In those areas, economic analysis is a powerful tool that brings a strong influence to bear on policy debates.

Currently, the main topic of debate within European policy circles is the Convention on the Future of Europe that was set up by the Laeken summit of the European Council in December 2001. The Convention could play a historic role comparable to the Philadelphia Convention of 1787 that drafted the US constitution. At the heart of the Convention is indeed work on a 'Constitutional Treaty' that would merge existing Treaties but most importantly overhaul the institutional system for the governance of Europe. The Convention is reviewing and preparing proposals for improving the mechanisms by which legislative, executive and judicial decision-making is taking place in Europe.

The need to reform the governance of Europe has been voiced repeatedly and increasingly in the past ten years. The looming enlargement of Europe by ten new member states by 2004 decided at the Copenhagen summit (Cyprus, Czech Republic, Estonia, Hungary, Latvia, Lithuania, Malta, Poland, Slovak Republic, Slovenia) has created a sense of urgency. There is a widespread consensus that the current institutions, initially created for a Europe of six member states, will no longer be adequate for a Union of twenty-five countries and more. The Nice Treaty made decisions relative to the number of commissioners, the number of members of the European Parliament (MEPs) and the decision weights of member states in the European Council. However, it was generally perceived that Nice delayed the more difficult but more substantial questions related to the governance of Europe. Enlargement makes reform more urgent because the inherent weaknesses of today's EU institutions risk being strongly magnified in a bigger Union of twenty-five. There could be a substantial risk of institutional collapse of the whole European construction of the past fifty years. Despite the apprehension in many countries of the risks posed by the uncertain prospects of reform of Europe's governance, the EU is seen as a major success story and apparently the time is ripe for such deep reforms.

What can economists say about the governance problem in Europe? Is this an area of expertise reserved exclusively for political scientists and scholars of constitutional law? In this chapter, I build on the recent literature in political economics (for a survey, see Persson and Tabellini, 2000, forthcoming) that analyses the economic effect of different political constitutions. That literature is still very new but it can shed light on the problems of the governance of Europe debated at the Convention.

In this chapter, I will not focus at all on competences of the Union but on governance issues: for those competences that are centralized at the European level, how should political decision-making (legislative and executive) be organized? What are the tradeoffs between different forms of political governance and what would be the optimal solution for an enlarged Europe? The issue of governance itself cannot be completely separated from the competences that should be exercised at the Union level, and the judgement on the most adequate form of governance depends on the kinds of public goods that one expects will be delivered at the European level. My working assumption, which I will justify below, will be that the enlarged EU will retain its current competences but will or should make significant progress in areas related to foreign policy and justice and home affairs.

In the second section, I go over the issues at stake in the drafting of the European Constitution. The Convention has already reached remarkable consensus on many points, but the issues of how to appoint the European executive and of the checks and balances between various European institutions is far from settled. In the third section, I review the relevant literature in political economics, analysing in particular the tradeoffs between parliamentary and presidential governance. In the fourth section, I argue in favour of presidential governance, with the president elected by an electoral college composed of national parliaments. I argue against the election of the president of the Commission by the European Parliament (EP) but also against the setting-up of a European Congress proposed by Giscard d'Estaing, the chairman of the Convention, and against a 'double executive' with a president of the Council elected by heads of state and a Commission president. Executive powers of the Commission must be strengthened, but so must its accountability both to the member states and to the citizens of Europe.

The issues at stake in the governance of Europe

The institutions created by the founding fathers of Europe have been the source of remarkable success in the last decades.

The success of Europe

The single market has expanded since 1957 both geographically (from six to fifteen, and soon to be twenty-seven) and in depth via the 1985 programme set in motion by Jacques Delors and European monetary union (EMU). This has brought decades of relative prosperity compared to the previous decades, which were characterized by the two most bloody wars in world history. The introduction of euro notes and coins in 2002 has generally been considered a success. Despite some localized price hikes, the euro's introduction was very smooth and European citizens have adapted to it remarkably quickly.

The EU has played a substantial role in stabilizing the macroeconomic situation in Europe, especially in the 1980s and 1990s. After World War II, the main European economies, the UK, France and Italy, followed very divergent paths. The EU has counteracted important government failures in individual countries and helped to create convergence at low levels of inflation. Without the EU, conditions in Belgium and Italy, for example, may eventually have resulted in Argentinian-type situations. This should be remembered in the context of the problems with the Growth and Stability Pact.

The co-operation of EU countries in EU integration has created a framework of peace within Europe after centuries of wars among the biggest European powers. Peace is one of the main objectives of the EU. Peace is achieved not only via more trade (the internal market), but also by EU members sharing increasingly common goals and values. EU countries will not wage wars against each other. Moreover, conflicts between countries are managed within the EU institutions (the BSE or 'mad cow disease' crisis, the dioxin scandal and so forth) which allow for dialogue and sometimes decisions by EU institutions that indicate an effective transfer of sovereignty to the EU. Enlargement holds the promise of peace on the broader European continent.

The EU has provided an institutional anchor that has allowed Greece, Spain and Portugal to achieve a successful transition from dictatorship to democracy. Participation in the EU has also been a very useful vehicle for modernization in these countries. Europe offers a similar future for potential new entrants who went through decades of Soviet occupation and economic stagnation in the socialist economic system. It is not an exaggeration to say that the favourable example of Europe played a positive role in the third wave of democratization in the final twenty years of the twentieth century.

If we compare the EU to any other supranational institution, such as the UN or the WTO, we must conclude that it has functioned more successfully than these other organizations. This is due to the 'méthode communautaire', or Community method, whereby the European Commission, responsible for promoting further economic integration, has had the responsibility (and also the exclusive right) continuously to initiate European legislative proposals, while the unanimity rule allowed countries to preserve their sovereignty.

The Commission, despite its very small size (an administration of fewer than 20,000 civil servants), has also played a very useful role in its competition policy, forcing national governments to undo decisions that conflicted with the Treaty of Rome. National governments have tended to abide by the decisions of the Commission. Decisions by the Court of Justice in the same direction have also been helpful. The precedence of European law in these matters has been more and more recognized and decisions of the Court and the Commission have generally been enforced. This is surprising, given the fact that the EU lacks any enforcement agencies and relies on national governments and bureaucracies for enforcement of its decisions.

Challenges ahead

In a way, the European Union is a victim of its own success. The past ten years have not only seen the number of member states and candidates to accession increase dramatically but also there has been a dramatic expansion of new areas of integration such as common foreign and security policy, and justice and home affairs. There is also, however, the clear perception that European institutions are not prepared to face the new and important challenges in those areas.

Suppose a shock like 11 September – such as a bombing of EU buildings in Brussels or the ECB buildings in Germany, or co-ordinated terrorist attacks in several major European cities – were to affect the EU. If the EU were not able to react swiftly, got bogged down in endless negotiations between countries and revealed to the outside world its failure to solve its 'collective action' problem, the ensuing loss in legitimacy could be lethal for the whole project of European integration. The comparison with the decisive reaction of the United States in the weeks after the 11 September attack could deeply discredit the EU institutions. The EU survived its inability to deal appropriately with the Yugoslavia crisis. What would happen if there were a severe crisis, say between Slovakia and Hungary? If the EU is not ready and able to deal with important foreign policy or security shocks, the result of forty-five years of patient work of European integration could be lost for a very long time. There is in particular the need for a strong but legitimate and accountable executive at the EU level. This should clearly be one of the most important goals for the Convention, but it is also one of the most difficult to achieve.

Apart from such extreme though not unlikely scenarios, Europe also needs to have its voice heard in the world. A set of common European values is slowly emerging. While most of these values are held in common with the rest of the Western world (freedom and democracy), specific values are developing throughout Europe, such as opposition to the death penalty and a greater sense of solidarity, which is inspired by both social democracy and Christian conservatism. The need for Europe's voice to be heard in the world also points to the necessity of a legitimate and accountable executive.

These are clearly not the only challenges, but they are in my view the most important ones. While progress is still needed on the front of economic integration, it is fair to say that the most important legislative work is behind us rather than ahead. Enforcement of the single market will obviously remain important and that also is a matter of executive power. These remarks remain crucial. They imply that in the design of the new European governance one must pay special attention to the executive aspects.

The Laeken declaration and the Convention

The Laeken declaration of December 2001 decided the establishment of a Convention to prepare the next intergovernmental conference of 2004. In addition to its chairman and two vice-chairmen, the Convention is composed of:

- fifteen representatives of the governments of the member states,
- thirteen representatives of governments of countries candidate for accession,
- thirty representatives of the national parliaments,
- twenty-six representatives of the national parliaments of accession candidates,
- sixteen members of the European Parliament, and
- two representatives of the European Commission.

The Laeken declaration raised a number of questions for the Convention to answer. The Laeken declaration sought to:

- clarify the competences of the Union and the member states;
- ensure that the principle of subsidiarity is enforced and that creeping centralization of the competences of the Union is avoided;
- simplify the Union's instruments and reduce their number;
- create a constitution for European citizens; and
- increase democratic legitimacy and transparency. Some of the important issues raised in this last context are:
  - how to appoint the Commission president,
  - the extension of powers of the European Parliament,
  - a review of the electoral rules for the European Parliament,
  - how to clarify the legislative and executive role of Council,
  - how to ensure transparency of Council meetings,
  - how to ensure a balance between the various European institutions,

- ○ how to better involve national parliaments in the European decision-making process, and
- ○ how to achieve more effective decision-making (extension of qualified majority voting, simplification of the co-decision procedure, what to do with the rotating six-month presidency).

By the end of 2002, the Convention had been at work for more than six months and many of these questions have already been clarified and are the object of consensus.

On the issue of competences, an agreement has emerged rather quickly within the Convention against the idea of trying to compile an exhaustive catalogue of competences. Indeed, such a task would be nearly impossible. In economic terms, this would be tantamount to trying to write a complete contract. Indeed, areas of competence are always aggregate objects and they often overlap with each other. The Convention has understood very quickly that what matters is to ensure good institutional mechanisms both to allow further integration in certain areas if needed and to enforce subsidiarity.

There is nevertheless a broad consensus on keeping exclusive competence of the Union in areas such as trade policy, competition policy and monetary policy, as well as on the need to strengthen Europe's foreign policy and to have one voice speak for Europe. Agreement has been similarly achieved in the Convention on the need to have European cross-border action, especially in the areas of asylum and migration, to give operational powers to Europol and to establish democratic scrutiny of the latter.

Consensus also exists on very important topics like the insertion of the charter of fundamental rights in the Constitutional Treaty, the adoption of a single legal personality for the EU,[1] the merger of the Treaties and the need for a European Constitution.

There is broad agreement on the need for transparency in the legislative proceedings of Council meetings. Qualified majority voting should be extended to all areas in which the co-decision procedure applies.[2] The co-operation procedure should be abolished.

---

[1] Currently, international agreements between the EU and third countries must be signed by legal authorities of all member states.
[2] These are essentially the internal market, social policy, consumer protection and the environment.

The Convention has endorsed the conclusions of the working group on subsidiarity that proposed the establishment of an early warning system, whereby the Commission, together with the Council and the European Parliament, would have to inform the national parliaments of its legislative proposals. National parliaments would have six weeks to evaluate whether or not the proposals violate the principle of subsidiarity. If a sufficient number of national parliaments express such a judgement, the Commission would have to reconsider its proposals. This is seen as an 'ex ante' political judgement on subsidiarity taking the form of a 'yellow card'.

On the issue of legal instruments, the working group of the Convention on their simplification has proposed a reduction in the number of legal instruments from fifteen to five. They propose to call the current 'regulations' 'laws'. These are legislative decisions that are binding for all member states and are immediately applicable. The current category of European 'directive' should be renamed 'framework law'. These legislative decisions are also binding, but the choice of the form of implementation is left to the member states. They propose to introduce a category of 'decision', which would be binding but would not especially have an addressee. It is seen as a very flexible instrument since it may not necessarily be of application for all countries. The non-binding instruments (recommendations and opinions) would remain as they are now.

There also seems to be general agreement that the 'open method of co-ordination', i.e., a concerted action of member states outside the specified competences of the EU, should be defined in the Constitutional Treaty.

It should be stressed that these changes in themselves will represent a fundamental milestone in the history of the European Union, and they are very likely to go through. Nevertheless, there is still an absence of consensus on quite fundamental aspects of the future governance of Europe. Prime Minister Blair (UK) and President Chirac (France) have proposed that the six-month rotating presidency be replaced by a five-year president elected by the European Council. The proposal has been backed by Prime Minister Aznar of Spain. Giscard d'Estaing, the Convention chair, has also expressed support for this measure and has proposed the creation of a European Congress that would meet once a year to discuss the legislative agenda of the Commission. These proposals are seen as an offensive to make Europe more intergovernmentalist and to weaken the Commission and the European Parliament, the two most 'federalist' institutions. The federalist camp, composed mostly of the smaller countries, Germany and the main European parties represented in the European Parliament, consider that the election of a European president would create a power structure parallel to the European Commission. Also, the creation of a new institution, the European Congress, is seen as dangerous because it would destroy the existing balance between the institutions. The federalists have recommended the maintenance of current institutions and the election of the president of the Commission by the European Parliament in order to increase the accountability of the Commission. They propose to establish a system of 'double hat' whereby the president of the Commission would also act as chair of the Council. Belgian prime minister Guy Verhofstadt has made this idea more precise by stating that executive Councils should be chaired by the Commission and that legislative Councils should elect their own chair, as in all legislative assemblies.

The ideas of the 'federalist' camp are criticized in turn by the intergovernmentalists. They claim that the president of the Commission cannot be elected by the European Parliament because the latter is not legitimate enough. Voter turnout for the European Parliament is much lower than for national elections and it has not been increasing despite the stronger powers allocated to the European Parliament. This is a bit of a chicken-and-egg problem. Lack of interest by the general public in the European Parliament is very much related to its lack of powers. At the same time, reluctance to give more power to the European Parliament is usually justified by invoking the low interest of public opinion in its activities. Another argument is that European parties are not yet strong enough and cannot impose discipline on their members. This argument is often overstated. Econometric analysis of voting in the European Parliament shows that MEPs vote mainly along European party lines, and that European party cohesion has been increasing over time as the European Parliament received more powers, while country cohesion was low and decreasing (Noury and Roland, 2002; Hix, Noury and Roland, 2002). Nevertheless, national parliaments and governments are still clearly seen as the main source of legitimacy for the European electorates.

The above points need to be settled in a satisfactory way. Neither the 'intergovernmentalist' nor the 'federalist' position is likely to prevail as such. A good constitution should attempt to balance the concerns expressed on both sides. On the other hand, there is a big danger of a compromise emerging 'satisfying' concerns on both sides but producing a flawed institutional set-up. This will most likely be the biggest danger to avoid.

The fundamental tradeoff in European governance

The fundamental tradeoff within European institutions has always been on one hand to avoid the collective action problem or free riding of national governments in the provision of Europe-wide public goods, while on the other hand respecting the national sovereignty of member states.

This has been achieved in an ingenious way in the past decades with the Community method. Its basic principles are as follows. The European Commission is the agenda-setter for legislative proposals: that is, the Commission has the sole right to initiate proposals that are submitted to and voted upon in the Council. Traditionally, until the 1980s at least, most voting in the Council was by unanimity. Even when voting by majority was introduced, individual countries could always invoke the *Luxembourg compromise*, allowing individual countries to block a decision if they felt it threatened their national sovereignty. Though there have been major extensions of majority voting, major decisions in the EU are still taken by unanimity, and consensus is generally sought even when unanimity is not required.

The main advantage of the Community method is that the Commission, as guardian of the Treaty, has the task of constantly generating legislative proposals for further European integration. Resources necessary to generate legislative proposals are not huge. However, they require technical expertise (at the level of ministerial cabinets), a scarce resource. Cabinet staff in national governments are generally overworked and jump from one issue to the other depending on the political mood. The European Commission, seen as a legislative proposal-making institution, gathers strong expertise (legal, economic, political, technical) from all European countries. The quality of higher-level Commission staff is certainly comparable to, if not higher than, that in the cabinets of individual country governments. This small body of high-level technocrats has accumulated expertise and knowledge, allowing it to constantly generate proposals for further European integration. The Commission, having as its tasks to protect the Treaties and to foster European integration, has thus served very usefully as an instrument to prevent the pitfall of free riding in generating proposals. When the Second (common security and foreign policy) and Third Pillar (justice and home affairs) were introduced in the Amsterdam Treaty but excluded from the Community method reserved for the First Pillar (the single market and economic integration), the member states did not take a very active role in generating legislative proposals in those areas. This failure has led to demands to abandon the pillar system. The Commission has proved to be an efficient instrument for generating legislative proposals: the successes of European integration so far are mostly due to the Commission's efforts.

Not only has the Commission helped to prevent free riding in generating proposals but it has also managed to establish in general a relationship of trust with governments of member states. This is because the Commission has acted as a technocratic body with no political bias either to the left or to the right. Its only bias was supposed to be pro-European. This is very important. If legislative proposals had come from member countries or from European political parties, they would have been greeted with suspicion and would have met with much more opposition. Since the only bias of the Commission was pro-European, governments of member states needed only to check whether the Commission's proposals were congruent with or opposed to their national interest.

Simultaneously, the strong veto powers of the Council have always served as a powerful counterbalance to ensure that national interests were not hurt by European legislation. The Community method has worked well because the veto powers of the Council allow, as in the intergovernmental method, each country to make sure that its interests are not damaged while preventing free riding in generating proposals.

While the fundamental tradeoff between free riding and the preservation of national interests has been managed rather efficiently by the Community method in the past decades, it has developed non-negligible drawbacks.

The most important is the so-called democratic deficit. The Commission is currently appointed by the European Council. Voters thus have no real influence on the nomination of the Commission. Compared to presidential systems, the Commission is not directly elected by voters. Compared to parliamentary systems, the Commission is not formed by a majority coalition of parties that have won election to the European Parliament. There is no link at all between the results of the election in the European Parliament and the formation of the Commission, which is decided entirely by the Council.

European citizens thus do not have any direct influence on decision-making in the EU, except for the election of the European Parliament. However, the latter has fewer powers than normal legislatures in either a presidential or a parliamentary system. The democratic deficit is related to the fact that the Community method of legislative decision-making has so far relied on the political neutrality of the Commission. This neutrality is consistent with the weak legitimacy of the Commission. The body the EU countries choose to initiate legislative proposals needs to be consensual and not politically (or ideologically) partisan, so that Council members (either left or right) do not feel any bias against their own government. This neutrality, however, conflicts with demands of normal democratic institutions, whereby elections serve to indicate shifts in the preferences of the electorate. Such shifts are represented in the EP and in national governments following national elections, but not in the Commission. Moreover, the Commission is not directly accountable to citizens. The Commission cannot be punished in elections. The EP can oust the Commission but does not have the power of investiture in forming the Commission.

The problem of the democratic deficit will only get worse with enlargement. To EU citizens, Brussels will seem even farther away than it is now. It will also be magnified with the necessary integration of foreign policy, defence and internal security in the executive powers in the EU. It is unthinkable to vest executive powers in the Commission in those areas without strong mechanisms of accountability both to European citizens and to European governments. This is certainly one of the main reasons why common foreign and security policy and justice and home affairs were not made subject to the Community method when they were inserted in the Amsterdam Treaty as 'additional pillars'. Similarly, the nomination of a higher representative for foreign and security policy under the authority of the Council was also a departure from the traditional Community method. These developments of recent years show a contradictory trend. On one hand, there is a clear need for further integration but, on the other hand, the lack of legitimacy of existing institutions has led to anarchic institutional developments that are not sustainable in the long run.

In the debates on the Constitutional Treaty, the democratic deficit drives most proposals both from the 'intergovernmentalist' and from the 'federalist' camp. The intergovernmentalists want to take power away from the Commission because it lacks democratic legitimacy, and put it in the hands of the Council. The federalists, on the other hand, want to remedy the democratic deficit by having the Commission president elected by the European Parliament.

Proposals from either side risk destroying the institutional balance between pan-European and national interests that has been behind the success of European integration so far. Weakening the Commission could stall the engine of European integration at a critical moment, when it is important to make enlargement work and when there is an acute need for a European external and internal security policy. On the other hand, 'forcing' European integration against national sovereignties could lead to a loss of legitimacy that could severely damage the credibility of European institutions as a whole.

The challenge of the Convention is thus to find a more democratic and accountable set of institutions while keeping an adequate balance between both pan-European interests and national sovereignties.

Comparative politics and economic analysis

There are two main forms of democratic regimes: presidential and parliamentary. Recent research in political economics has highlighted the effect of the characteristic distinctions between these two types of political regime.

The main difference between presidential and parliamentary regimes is that, under the former, the executive is elected independently from the legislature (usually by universal suffrage) and cannot be deposed by a vote of no confidence. Under a parliamentary regime, the executive is chosen by the legislature, where it usually enjoys a majority support. The executive is not always formed by parties having a majority of seats in the parliament, since it is possible to have minority governments – as is often the case in Scandinavian countries – but the parliament has the power to bring down the executive by a vote of no confidence.

This distinction leads to two important characteristics that have an effect on policy-making. First, under a presidential regime, one can have stronger *separation of powers* between the legislative and executive branch of government compared to a parliamentary regime. This is indeed the case in the world's best-known presidential regime, the United States. Executive powers are vested in the president's office. Many of the executive's powers are, however, subject to checks by the legislature such as the approval of the signature of international treaties, executive appointments, etc. Moreover, in legislative matters, agenda-setting powers reside with the legislative branch of government, not the executive branch, though the latter can exercise certain veto rights. Agenda-setting powers are thus devolved to legislative committees. This institutional set-up makes it possible to have, among other things, 'divided government', with the executive being controlled by one party and the legislature being controlled by another, as has often been the case in the United States over the past twenty years. Obviously, the degree of separation of powers in presidential systems depends on the constitution itself, and many presidential regimes feature very little separation of powers (see Shugart and Carey, 1992 for the most complete analysis of presidential democracies to date). Such a separation of powers cannot take place in a parliamentary system. Indeed, the powers of the executive emanate from the legislature and not from an independent source. This implies that executives necessarily control the legislature since otherwise they could not stay in power. The executive thus controls a majority of votes and therefore also has de facto enormous agenda-setting powers. Moreover, it can use the cabinet resources to generate legislative proposals.

This distinction between presidential and parliamentary systems also has another implication: *legislative cohesion* of the majority in power in parliamentary systems. In other words, the majority in the parliament approves the legislative proposals emanating from the government in a very disciplined way, while the opposition generally votes against. Such legislative cohesion is less strong in presidential systems. There, voting majorities form more on a case-by-case basis. The reason for the strong legislative cohesion in parliamentary regimes, put forward using game-theoretic tools by Huber (1996) and Diermeier and Feddersen (1998), lies precisely in the existence of the vote of confidence in that regime. Indeed, the government can always associate a vote of confidence with a legislative bill, so that if the bill is defeated the government is censured. This threat allows the disciplining of the parties of the government coalition. Indeed, since a deviation from coalition discipline can be punished by a vote of no confidence in which the incumbent coalition would lose its agenda-setting powers and be replaced by another, coalition partners have an incentive to vote together. In a presidential system, the absence of a vote of confidence removes this disciplining device. Therefore, voting behaviour by individual representatives tends to be less disciplined and based more on the perception of the interests of their local constituencies.

These two important characteristics of political regimes have an impact on policy-making and economic outcomes, as shown by Persson, Roland and Tabellini (2000), and these give rise to interesting tradeoffs.

In a parliamentary regime, the existence of legislative cohesion favours the funding of broad expenditure programmes for public goods or of transfer programmes that benefit large majorities. However, it is also a machine for collusion that allows politicians jointly to reap rents using their privileged position in power. This should lead to the provision of more public goods, but also to more corruption and to government being bigger.

Presidential systems that lack such legislative cohesion tend to produce legislation that favours more narrowly targeted expenditure programmes, benefiting local constituencies of particular representatives. At the same time, it is possible to have budgetary procedures that create conflicts of interest between different political agents. For example, the president or a legislative committee may use powers to propose a small budget knowing that the budget process will be diverted towards specific local interests and rents to politicians. This separation of powers reduces the size of the government budget as well as rents to politicians. The prediction is therefore that presidential systems with separation of powers should have fewer public goods and more particularistic local goods, but that the total size of the budget should be smaller and there should be less corruption.

Empirical research on the difference between parliamentary and presidential regimes (Persson and Tabellini, 2003 forthcoming) has confirmed that the weight of government in the economy of the latter, measured as spending by government, is at least 5 per cent of GDP lower, a non-negligible amount. Government spending in presidential democracies is also less persistent and less responsive to unexpected shocks. Parliamentary democracies, especially those with proportional representation, tend to have an increasing trend in budgetary expenditures and larger welfare programmes.

This research is only in its initial phases. One aspect that may be important in the European context is that, in presidential regimes, voting on a case-by-case basis makes it less likely to be systematically in the minority. Other aspects are important and have not been the subject of study: is the executive likely to be of higher quality under a presidential regime or not? How well do presidential regimes and parliamentary regimes deal with ethnic and linguistic heterogeneity? Some answers to those questions will obviously be necessary in the European context.

Tradeoffs between presidential and parliamentary regimes in the context of Europe

Most European countries are parliamentary democracies.[3] Even the semi-presidential European countries (France and Finland) are much more similar to the parliamentary model than to a fully presidential democracy such as the United States. In the current debate in the Convention, it seems that the most likely direction is a parliamentary model. Indeed, as seen above, the main debate on the appointment of the European executive is between intergovernmentalists, who wish to have a president of the European Council elected by the Council, and the federalists, who generally wish to have the president of the Commission elected by the European Parliament. Various proposals routinely include the right of the Parliament (and sometimes also of the Council) to censure the Commission. These are thus proposals to adopt the parliamentary model. The debates are not, however, couched in terms of choice between the presidential and the parliamentary model, but in terms of 'federalist' versus 'intergovernmentalist' institutions.

A move towards a parliamentary system would be very simple to organize. All that is needed is to give the Parliament instead of the Council the right of initiative in forming the Commission. The most complete form of a parliamentary control over the Commission would give the European Parliament the power to appoint the *whole* Commission. The political composition of the Commission would then reflect proportionality between party groups of a coalition that represents a majority in the EP. This would definitely 'politicize' the Commission along the left–right dimension. According to the parliamentary logic,

---

[3] Many of the ideas in this section are borrowed from a CEPR report co-authored with Erik Berglöf, Barry Eichengreen, Guido Tabellini and Charles Wyplosz (Berglöf *et al.*, 2003). Many other ideas in this paper have benefited from discussion with them.

a 'Commission coalition' could also be brought down by a vote of no confidence in the Parliament between two elections and be replaced by another coalition.

A parliamentary model for Europe

What would be the benefits and drawbacks of a parliamentary form of governance in the specific context of the European Union?

Among the benefits, accountability would certainly improve. Elections for the Parliament would be elections for the Commission just as parliamentary elections in member states are elections for the government. Elections to the Parliament would thus be less like 'national protest votes' than today, since the electorate would have the power to determine the political orientation of the coalition. The electorate would also have the power to punish Europarties that have misbehaved in power.

More power to the European Parliament should have the effect of increasing cohesion of 'Europarties' inside the EP as suggested by the econometric evidence (Noury and Roland, 2002). Representation of European socioeconomic groups, capital, labour and the middle class would thus be better assured. Electoral campaigns would put forward EU-wide issues of interest to the broadest categories of voters. Representation of countries would still be assured in two ways: (a) the veto power in the Council with supermajority thresholds; (b) country representation in the Commission as decided in Nice. Such country representation in the Commission with one representative per country is clearly inefficient. However, in the parliamentary model, the Commission would be elected indirectly by the European Parliament, so pressures for representatives from each country in the Commission (or for some form of rigid rotation) would be nearly irresistible.

A parliamentary model would also carry many obvious disadvantages in the context of Europe. Even if the Commission has increased powers, the constraint of having one commissioner per country – difficult to escape in the absence of direct elections – would possibly have a negative impact on efficiency. The inefficiency is caused not only by the large number of commissioners, but also by the fact that the Commission is a very proportional body. Given the heterogeneity of voter preferences across countries, any coalition in the Commission would require more than two parties, possibly three or four. Smaller parties would carry considerable hold-up power within the Commission, as would country representatives threatening to resign. Such threats could be effective because they jeopardize the survival of the incumbent coalition and lead to a government crisis similar to those observed in parliamentary governments with large coalition governments in the past (the French Fourth Republic, the Italian First Republic and post-war Belgium). One commissioner from a small party in a small country could thus hold up the Commission. A resignation (when the Commission does not give in) would necessarily lead to multiple cabinet reshuffles in order to maintain the fragile balances, undermining any executive powers the Commission may be given over areas, such as foreign and internal policy, in which the ability to respond swiftly in crisis situations is critical. The lack of efficiency may be harmful to legitimacy.

Of course, the situation would be different if the Commission were a single-party government, as in the UK, for example. However, any parliamentary governance of Europe is unlikely to resemble the UK Westminster model. The first reason is that the first-past-the-post system does not necessarily lead to broad representation of constituencies within the government. A second and more important reason is that majoritarian elections are not likely to lead to single-party government (Persson, Roland and Tabellini, 2003 in progress). Indeed, given the political heterogeneity in Europe, it is quite likely that the first-past-the-post system would lead to a dominance of single parties at the level of countries or regions but not at the level of Europe. Indeed, if voters in various countries and regions of Europe have diverse loyalties to the different European parties, a first-past-the-post system would mainly lead to the election of the party that commands the most loyalty in each electoral constituency. Majoritarian elections would then not necessarily lead to a two-party system ('Duverger's law'), but in all likelihood still result in coalition governments. These would, however, function even less well than coalition governments elected under proportional rules. Indeed, the core constituencies of various parties would be well-defined geographical rather than socioeconomic constituencies. Conflicts inside the coalition would then probably turn on geographical interests, as is already the case in the Council. One may then end up without any EU institutions that cater to pan-European interests. The point of this argument is mainly that majoritarian electoral rule is neither likely nor desirable for elections to the European Parliament. Thus, in all likelihood, a parliamentary system would be based on proportional representation and the Commission would be a form of coalition government.

To summarize the discussion, the parliamentary model described above would thus be good for obtaining European-wide public goods provision but the probability of coalition governments has disadvantages in terms of efficiency of executive tasks, an important problem in external and internal security. These two basic properties will be present in any parliamentary model. However, the basic institutional details may mean that things move in the right or in the wrong direction.

First, the risk of a crisis depends to a certain extent on the rules for the vote of no confidence. Here, research tends to show that the German-style 'constructive vote of no confidence' is more desirable than other methods (Diermeier, Eraslan and Merlo, 2003 forthcoming). Indeed, the specificity of that rule is that a government can be brought down only if there is an alternative majority coalition available to govern. This has two advantages. First, this avoids protracted periods of government crisis (and lengthy negotiations for government formation with caretaker governments), which are often observed in countries with coalition government. Second, it makes it less easy to bring down a government, since agreeing on an alternative coalition is often very difficult. Germany has had few government crises thanks to this mechanism. Belgium, traditionally known for the short duration of its governments, has had no government crisis since this rule was introduced in the early 1990s.

Second, the disadvantage of potential conflicts within a coalition government and their negative effects on executive tasks could be mitigated by insulating the president of the Commission (and possibly vice-presidents with important executive tasks in trade, common security and foreign policy, and justice and home affairs) from a vote of no confidence. This would be a version of the current Israeli political model in which, although the prime minister is elected for the whole legislature and cannot be ousted by the Knesset, his coalition can be voted down. In effect, this would be a form of presidential model. Let us now turn the discussion to the latter.

A presidential model for Europe

In a fully fledged presidential model, the Commission president, or part of the Commission (the president and a certain number of vice-presidents), would be directly elected by European citizens. Such a Commission would have well-defined executive powers in a limited number of areas to be made more precise, but they would have to include foreign policy representation, policing powers within the EU and some (obviously very limited) military powers. In the most complete version of presidential democracy, the president of the Commission would have full power over the appointment and the removal of individual commissioners, possibly subject to specific rules of representation of countries or general guidelines over appointment criteria. Any realistic scenario of an elected Commission president implies that his powers would necessarily be limited.

There would be several advantages to such 'presidential' governance. First, accountability would be very strong. European voters would have direct power over the election and re-election of that constrained executive, dramatically reducing the democratic deficit. Europe and its policies would be 'the' salient issue when voters appoint him. The strength of the US Constitution is that the legitimacy of the executive derives from the voters. 'We the people . . .' were the most controversial words in the draft American constitution because they meant that the executive was to be directly elected by the people and not by the state legislatures. Direct competition among potential leaders of Europe would certainly give parties a stronger incentive to choose candidates with great leadership potential. Accountability would be stronger in the presidential than in the parliamentary model. Indeed, incumbents would have to face voters directly to seek re-election. In the parliamentary model, this mechanism is indirect. It is weakened by the list system generally associated with parliamentary systems. It is further undermined by the fact that centrist parties in coalition governments are often needed to form a majority. Even if these parties are punished by voters and lose seats, they are nevertheless greatly insulated from sanctions by the electorate.

A big advantage of the presidential model is that the executive would be better able to react swiftly in times of crisis without facing the danger of a government crisis or inefficient wars of attrition within the executive (see Alesina and Drazen, 1991). Checks on the executive by the Council and the Parliament also ensure representation indirectly via veto powers of these bodies.

One big problem with presidential governance might be related to representation. Assume that each of the most relevant parties within the EU (the conservatives, the socialists, the liberals, the greens) propose a candidate for president. It is quite possible that the winner (most likely a socialist or a conservative) would be elected despite representing only around 30 per cent of voters. In other words, the elected representative would represent too few interests. This is easy to remedy, however, by having a runoff system, as in the French presidential elections. A runoff allows only two candidates to go to the second round and ensures that at least 50 per cent of the voters would be represented by the winning candidate. The first round will continue to provide information about changes in the preferences of the electorate and helps to reveal the relative strength of various Europarties (Piketty, 2000; Castanheira, 1998). The French system could be improved in the European context by having each of the two top candidates from the first round come up with a team of vice-presidents (say four: with responsibilities for defence, foreign policy, justice and home affairs, and trade). Having two teams competing directly in front of the electorate would have several advantages. First, each candidate would be careful to have an adequate geographical representation in his team. Second, and this is probably a big advantage over a parliamentary model, parties would have incentives to choose strong personalities recognized by the electorate and not tarnished by previous experience of incompetence or mismanagement. The direct election of the Commission presidents and vice-presidents in a runoff system could be positive for representation. The fear is often expressed, especially in small countries, that with direct presidential elections only candidates from big countries would have a chance of becoming president. However, this idea is unfounded. In a Europe of twenty-five member states, there is no clear arithmetic advantage to being a politician in a big country. What matters much more is a strong personality and an ability to show leadership.

There are, however, also disadvantages to a presidential model of governance. As seen above, coalitions in the legislature form on a vote-by-vote basis and internalize less the broad interests of the population, which leads to underprovision of public goods. This is a first drawback. There is indeed the risk that legislative activity could centre on pork barrel politics as in the US Congress. One may then end up with more programmes, like the common agricultural policy, targeted at narrow interests that may be pivotal in legislative votes. This problem is probably the most serious one with presidential governance.

This can be mitigated by introducing measures that strengthen the European party system. An easy solution is to give Europarties power to establish electoral lists. This is not without cost since the list system reduces accountability. Indeed, since parties choose the list, voters cannot vote down a politician who has misbehaved if his party has put him high on the list. Very often, the interests of parties and voters will be congruent and parties will not want to place unpopular politicians at the top of their list. However, some incompetent politicians might intrigue their way to a high place on the list and not have to fear voters. Despite this drawback, giving power over the list of candidates for the European Parliament to Europarties would be a powerful instrument for achieving party discipline. Having a strong party system within the EP would not eliminate vote-by-vote coalitions, but they would be coalitions based on Europarties rather than on narrow constituencies of pivotal MEPs, as is the case in the US Congress. This would thus bode better for public goods provision at the European level and would probably be enough to avoid the pitfalls of pork barrel politics of presidential systems.

Another potential problem with the presidential model of governance is related to the heterogeneity of languages within the EU. None of the EU politicians knows the languages of all EU countries. This situation will become even worse after enlargement. A candidate will be able to campaign effectively in those countries or regions of which he masters the language but not in others, which would realistically mean most of the member states. This important communication barrier between politicians and the population would mean that electoral campaigns take on a character very different from their current nature. This problem would be present in the parliamentary model too, but in presidential campaigns the personality of the candidates and their direct contact with the public is important. This problem is, however, not insurmountable. First, the electorate will have followed the track record of the incumbent and be able to vote to punish or reward him for it. One can also argue that track records of incumbents matter more than campaign promises since the latter are often not fulfilled anyway. Nevertheless, given the communication problem, for the presidential model to work well, pan-European parties need to acquire prominence. Candidates for the job of president should be chosen from within Europarties. In the scenario of a presidential 'team' outlined above, each of the two presidential candidates would choose members of his team among a coalition of Europarties, making the best possible geographical balance. Parties would thus play an important role in the selection of executive candidates and their local representation in the various countries would become vital in the communication between voters and candidates. Note that in India – a multicultural country where English is the communication language of the elite (but not of the population at large) – party organization plays a crucial role in communication and representation.

Comparing the parliamentary and the presidential models

If we compare the advantages and drawbacks of the parliamentary and the presidential modes of governance, which one do we find would be best suited for Europe?

The parliamentary model would produce strong legislative cohesion in the European Parliament. This would be propitious for legislating on the provision of broad public programmes that benefit a majority. On the other hand, strong legislative cohesion may lead to patterns of majority coalition in which certain countries and parties are systematically in the minority. The presidential system will suffer less from the danger of oppression of minorities since votes will be issue by issue. Moreover, the European Parliament will have the power to make real legislative choices which may help to enhance its public perception. The separation of powers that exists in the presidential system may thus be better suited for Europe. The disadvantage of the presidential system in terms of providing large public programmes such as the welfare system is not likely to be that important in the European context, because welfare systems are already strong in most European countries and there is no real evidence that they are being eroded by globalization or European integration. The presidential system would also be better from the point of view of accountability since the executive can be directly voted down; in the parliamentary system such a removal is possible only indirectly, via coalition formation in the legislature emerging from the elections. Moreover, under proportional representation, centrist parties tend to be in most coalitions even when voters punish them in the ballot box. Finally, executive effectiveness is clearly better under the presidential system than under a parliamentary system with coalition government. Executive effectiveness will be very important in areas of foreign policy and justice and home affairs. The conclusion is thus that a presidential form of governance would be better suited for Europe.

Note, however, that in either the presidential or the parliamentary scenario, it will be necessary to strengthen the European party system by at least giving the leaders of Europarties power to establish electoral lists. However, we do not know yet how effective such a change would be. We can only rely on the predictions of theory (and empirical evidence) but cannot be certain that Europarties will discipline their representatives as well as one would hope. In a parliamentary system, voting discipline is crucial for political stability, since the survival of the executive depends on it. In a presidential system, it is less important. This is an additional argument in favour of a presidential system. As shown in Noury and Roland (2002) and in Hix, Noury and Roland (2002), voting discipline in the European Parliament is currently already comparable to that in the US Congress, but is still significantly below that in parliamentary democracies.

In a presidential system, the European party system would have to be improved mainly for the selection of presidential candidates, every five years (to be in line with elections in the European Parliament). Indeed, one needs to avoid presidential races being between representatives of countries or groups of countries, and instead ensure that they are races between parties that are well represented in all European countries. For that purpose, it would be useful to introduce a rule stating that presidential candidates need, for example, the signature of a legislator from two-thirds of EU member states in order to compete. This means that the presidential race will be mainly between candidates chosen by political organizations with a widespread European presence. The choice of a candidate by parties may itself require a system of primaries as in the United States, but this is probably best left to the parties themselves. A great advantage of primaries is that they reveal the extent of public support for various candidates, a variable about which there will certainly be important uncertainty in the European context.

The European party system can also be improved by the correct timing of the elections. Simultaneous second-round elections for the presidency and the European Parliament, or elections for the latter following the presidential elections (as in France), would help to transform legislative elections into elections of support or opposition to the European president.

In any event, an elected European executive will need to be strongly constrained and subject to checks and balances from the European Parliament and from the Council. Checks by the Council will be especially important. Given that Europe is still, and will be for a long time, a supranational construction, the fundamental tradeoff between free riding and respect for national sovereignty must be solved in such a way that a desirable increase in the powers of the European executive must be associated with reassuring checks from national governments on the action of the executive. The model here for a European president, a European foreign minister and other executive functions should be that of the current relationship between the Council and the trade commissioner. Indeed, trade is an exclusive competence of the Union, and this is not disputed by anybody. Nevertheless, the trade commissioner, who has executive responsibility over European trade policy, constantly goes to the Council to get the green light for the actions he proposes, such as negotiations with the United States or with other groups of countries. Any action taken by the trade commissioner is thus subject to ex ante scrutiny by the Council. This does not mean that there is paralysis of decision-making. Rather, the trade commissioner, who has an accurate idea of the actions he wants to undertake, is checked by the Council in case one or several member states strongly disagree with the action proposed. This is a good system of checks and balances that should be replicated in the other executive functions of the Commission.

A president elected by national parliaments

However, it is too soon to imagine the election of the president of the Commission by universal suffrage. It is not even considered as one of the options by the Convention. However, a flexible path towards a presidential system would be to have the president elected by an electoral college as suggested by Hix (2002). Each country would have the right to a certain number of 'electoral college votes' that are proportional to its population, and would be able to determine how to allocate those votes. The idea would be that, in a first stage, electoral college votes in a country would be obtained by a vote in the national parliament. The electoral college votes would thus be proportional to the votes for the candidates in the national parliament.[4] Election of the president of the Commission by national parliaments is a very attractive solution.

[4] This detail is crucial if we want to avoid winner-take-all effects as in Florida in the 2000 US election. With proportionality, if one candidate gets 49 per cent of votes in the French parliament and another gets 51 per cent, then respectively 49 per cent and 51 per cent of France's electoral college vote should go to those candidates.

One of the themes of the Convention is increasing the role of national parliaments. The convention has so far not come up with important ideas in that area. What better role to give to the national parliaments than to vote for the president of the Commission? This would give the president both more legitimacy and also make him more accountable, since he would have to seek re-election. This solution also seems like a good compromise between the two currently most popular proposals, i.e., the election of the Commission president by the European Parliament, supported by Germany and the smaller countries, and the election of a Council president by the Council supported by Blair, Aznar and Chirac. Note that this would be an efficient rather than a flawed compromise. A big danger with the Blair/Chirac/Aznar proposal is that the Council presidency would form a rival source of power to the Commission and that this would create unnecessary clashes between the two that could weaken the EU institutions as a whole. I will return to this issue below.

On the other hand, the election of the president of the Commission by the European Parliament would be a step in the direction of a parliamentary model which, as seen above, is not the best for Europe. Election of the president by an electoral college initially formed by national parliaments would give democratic legitimacy and accountability to the European executive.

This proposal is not very different from the proposal to elect the Commission president by a European Congress formed of representatives from national parliaments and from the European Parliament. However, it has the big advantage of flexibility over the latter. There is no actual need to have all parliamentarians at the same place when voting for the president. Moreover, the electoral college option allows an evolution of the system towards universal suffrage. This is exactly what happened in the United States, where state legislators initially elected the president. In the early 1800s, over 60 per cent of the electoral college was chosen by state legislators. Only after 1824 did the role of state legislatures in presidential elections wane (see McCarty, 2002) in favour of direct suffrage.

Results from a counterfactual exercise

To put some data in the analysis, Simon Hix, Abdul Noury and I have done a counterfactual exercise to ask how the political composition of the Commission would compare to its actual composition over the past twenty years. We used roll call data in the European Parliament to calculate NOMINATE scores (Poole and Rosenthal, 1997) and estimate each MEP's ideal point on a two-dimensional space, where the first dimension represents the left–right spectrum and the second represents the pro–anti European aspect. We explored different scenarios explained in more detail in Hix, Noury and Roland (2003). The three most important ones are the following:

(1) In the first scenario, we asked what would have been the political affiliation of the Commission president if he had been elected by the Parliament. We assumed a multiple-round election in which the weakest candidate is eliminated at each round until a candidate has a majority of votes, a procedure that is much used in the EP. We assume party discipline on voting.

(2) In the second scenario, we wondered what would be the most likely coalition government in the Commission assuming that each party is chosen as formateur with probability equal to its share of seats in the EP, and that a formateur picks first as partner the party that is the closest to itself, but assuming a minimum winning coalition, i.e., smaller parties that are not necessary to reach 50 per cent can be dropped from the coalition.

(3) The last scenario assumes a two-round election for president in the national parliaments.

Table 1.1 gives the results of this exercise.

Several things are striking when one looks at table 1.1. First of all, one sees that only when the president of the Commission is elected by the national parliaments does one replicate the actual composition of the Commission over the past twenty years. This can be explained by the fact that elections in the European Parliament are often protest votes against the incumbents. Thus, while most governments in Europe were to the left in the late 1990s, the elections to the EP in 1999 gave a clear majority to the right. This means that if EP elections continue to be second-order contests and the president of the Commission is elected by the EP, he will start his mandate with a Council of a different political vintage. This is likely to create unnecessary clashes between the Commission and the Council. However, as discussed above, this effect is likely to be mitigated because voter behaviour should change if the European Parliament acquires more power. Second, a grand coalition

Table 1.1 *Counterfactual scenarios for the selection of the European executive*

	EP1, 1979	EP2, 1984	EP3, 1989	EP4, 1994	EP5, 1999
Real world					
Commission majority	(Jenkins+Thorn) Right	(Delors I) Right	(Delors II+III) Right	(Santer) Right	(Prodi) Left
Counterfactual analysis					
Election by EP of:					
Commission president (EP group voting)	Right (EPP)	Right (EPP)	Right (EPP)	Left (SOC)	Right (EPP)
Coalition government (50 per cent)	Grand coalition (SOC-EPP)	Left (SOC-LIB-LEFT)	Grand coalition (SOC-EPP)	Grand coalition (SOC-EPP)	Right (EPP-LIB-GAU)
Election by national parliament of:					
Commission president	Right (EPP)	Right (EPP)	Right (EPP)	Right (EPP)	Left (SOC)

Source: Hix, Noury and Roland (2003).

Note: EPP = European Popular Party (conservatives); GAU = Gaullists; LEFT = parties to the left of the Socialists, including former communists; LIB = Liberals; SOC = Socialists.

government including the two big parties, the Socialists and the Conservatives (EPP), is quite likely as it would have emerged in three of five legislatures. In 1984, one would have had a left-wing government including the radical left (mostly former communist parties). The Single Market Programme would probably not have passed under such circumstances. Any right- or left-wing government also will be formed by at least two parties as indicated in table 1.1. This counterfactual exercise makes the scenario of election of the president by the national parliaments even more attractive.

A comparison with existing proposals

The most prominent proposal is the one to replace the six-month ro- tating presidency by a president of the European Council elected every five years by the European Council as proposed by Prime Minister Blair, backed by Jacques Chirac and other European leaders (in partic- ular Giscard d'Estaing, the chairman of the Convention). He would be the 'president' of Europe and Europe's face to the outside world. He would also chair the biannual summits of the European Council. The high representative for foreign and security policy would act as the for- eign minister of the Union. He also would be chosen by the European Council. In legislative matters, the current system would stay in place. The Commission would keep its right of initiative and would propose legislation that should increasingly be approved by the co-decision pro- cedure between the European Parliament and the Council.

In isolation, the proposal sounds good. Indeed, replacing the six-month presidency by a five-year presidency would create more continuity in the agenda of the European Council. However, this pro- posal strengthens the power of the Council to the detriment of the Commission and the European Parliament, the only two institutions that are 'advocates for Europe'. The election of an EU president in the Council, especially if his powers go beyond chairing the Council meet- ings, would create overlap and rivalry with the post of the president of the Commission and risk an institutional clash between the Council president and the Commission president. The confusion between the ju- risdiction of the Council presidency and that of the Commission would possibly indeed lead to severe conflicts of competences. More impor- tantly, it would lead to a general weakening of the European executive and, mutatis mutandis, of EU institutions as a whole. A dynamic of further weakening the Commission could destroy all the wealth of expertise that has built up over the decades in that institution.

To some extent, the Blair–Chirac proposal reflects the concern that the Commission lacks democratic legitimacy. One should not forget that, ironically, the Commission is set up by the Council. Legitimacy of the Commission is, however, a genuine concern. The obvious solution is to make the Commission more accountable to Europe's citizenry rather than undermining it in favour of a 'new' form of European executive that would seriously alter the balance of the European institutions, with unpredictable consequences.

On the other hand, it is quite understandable that the heads of state would want to have closer control over new executive powers given to the Commission. As stated above, ex ante monitoring of executive action by the Council is an adequate solution. Checks and balances are the solution, not duplication of powers.

Similarly, the idea of a European Congress that would elect the president of the Commission and review the legislative plans and strategic orientations of the Commission's action on an annual basis seems like a good idea in isolation. However, there is a serious danger that its functions would clash with the current functions of the European Parliament. This institution would serve merely to rubber-stamp and hold general discussion if its role is as Giscard d'Estaing has defined it. It is not difficult to see that, once put in place, this institution would try to increase its powers. This can happen only to the detriment of the European Parliament, which has developed more than twenty years of expertise in European legislation. Moreover, MEPs are elected by universal suffrage. Many of them have been in national parliaments. Many are well-known political figures in their country. It is not clear why they would lack legitimacy and why the Congress would have more legitimacy. Moreover, as stated above, this Congress is not needed to elect the president of the Commission by the national parliaments.

Conclusion

In any event, whatever the outcome of the Convention, there are reasons to be optimistic about the institutional future of Europe. The Convention is an extremely useful institution, able to make a proposal for a constitution for Europe that should fit its best interests for the future. It goes much further than the previous intergovernmental conferences that were mainly a form of bargaining between countries where no one was there mainly to fight for the interests of Europe as compared to those of their own countries. The Convention comes also at the right time. After the successful Copenhagen summit of the end of 2002, which decided on the historic enlargement of Europe to twenty-five by 2004, it is clear that Europe's institutions must change for the better to cope with a Europe of twenty-five and more member states.

In conclusion, it is vital to outline the importance of an evolutionary approach to the constitution (see Berglöf *et al.*, 2003). Things can, of course, go wrong but they can also evolve in the right direction provided the constitution is not too much of a straitjacket. The writers of the Constitutional Treaty must distinguish between what is to last and what should evolve. What should last should be written clearly. What should evolve should not be written down in the constitution. For example, majority rules on legislation are likely to evolve over time. One should thus not write down specific majority rules for specific domains in the constitution. On the contrary, the constitution should state that the Council should decide on any change in the majority rule, which should then be subject to unanimity.

In any event, the strengthening of EU institutions will take time. Even under the best scenario, the EU executive will remain weak for decades. It will take a lot of practice and learning by doing, taking up new opportunities to strengthen the legitimacy of the European executive. Even the United States took more than half a century after its constitution was adopted before the executive played any significant role.

However, compared to Europe's past, the current changes are a quantum leap. Seen in historical perspective, the pace of progress of European integration is quite dazzling. It is very encouraging. European construction remains a challenge because of its rich multicultural diversity. The European Union has been a most successful example of a supranational organization that may be a role model for more ambitious projects of supranational organizations. Success in its current institutional change will, it is hoped, set a positive example which may be emulated elsewhere and lead to improvements in multinational governance in other regions of the world.

References

Alesina, A. and A. Drazen (1991), 'Why are stabilizations delayed?', *American Economic Review*, 81: 1170–1188.

Baldwin, Richard and Charles Wyplosz (2003 forthcoming), *The economics of European integration*.

Berglöf, Erik, Barry Eichengreen, Gérard Roland, Guido Tabellini and Charles Wyplosz (2003), *Built to last: A political architecture for Europe*, CEPR Report Monitoring the European Economy no. 12, London: Centre for Economic Policy Research.

Castanheira, Micael (1998), 'Voting for losers' (mimeo), European Centre for Advanced Research in Economics, Université Libre de Bruxelles.

Diermeier, Daniel, Hulya Eraslan and Antonio Merlo (2003 forthcoming), 'A structural model of government formation', *Econometrica*.

Diermeier, Daniel and Tim Feddersen (1998), 'Cohesion in legislatures and the vote of confidence procedure', *American Political Science Review*, 92: 611–621.

Hix, Simon (2002), *Linking national politics to Europe*, London: Foreign Policy Centre.

Hix, Simon, Abdul Noury and Gérard Roland (2002), 'Understanding the European Parliament: party cohesion and competition, 1979–2001' (mimeo), University of California, Berkeley.

(2003), 'How to choose the European executive: a counterfactual analysis 1979–1999' (mimeo), University of California, Berkeley.

Huber, John (1996), 'The impact of confidence votes on legislative politics in parliamentary systems', *American Political Science Review*, 90: 269–282.

McCarty, N. (2002), 'Presidential vetoes in the early Republic' (mimeo), Princeton University.

Noury, Abdul and Gérard Roland (2002), 'More power to the European Parliament?', *Economic Policy*, 34: 279–320.

Persson, Torsten, Gérard Roland and Guido Tabellini (2000), 'Comparative politics and public finance', *Journal of Political Economy*, 108: 1121–1161.

(2003), 'Comparative politics and electoral rules', work in progress.

Persson, Torsten and Guido Tabellini (2000), *Political economics: explaining economic policy*, Cambridge, MA: MIT Press.

(forthcoming), *The economic effect of constitutions*, Cambridge, MA: MIT Press.

Piketty, Thomas (2000), 'Voting as communicating', *Review of Economics Studies*, 67: 169–191.

Poole, Keith T. and Howard Rosenthal (1997), *Congress: a political-economic history of roll call voting*, Oxford: Oxford University Press.

Shugart, M. and J. Carey (1992), *Presidents and assemblies*, Cambridge: Cambridge University Press.

2 | Improving the performance of the European social model: the welfare state over the individual life cycle

ASSAR LINDBECK

Introduction

Welfare state arrangements are more comprehensive in Western Europe, or Europe for short, than in other parts of the world. As a result, welfare state spending (including expenditures on education) typically hovers at around 25–35 per cent of GDP among European countries (gross figures, OECD, 2002). The achievements are also impressive. In particular, there is considerable income security over the individual's life cycle, largely as a result of social insurance. Governments have also boosted the consumption of various types of (personal) social services with strong elements of investment in human capital – in particular, education and health care, as well as child care in some countries. Poverty has also been mitigated, not only as a result of social insurance but also via selective income support and social services that are made available for low-income groups. In countries where the children of low-income groups enjoy a relatively large share of aggregate education services, the factor incomes of these groups have also improved.

Some welfare state arrangements also contribute to favourable economic and social *dynamics*. For example, when aggregate investment in human capital is stimulated, future labour productivity is boosted, which in turn improves the future aggregate tax base. As a result, in a long-term perspective, these types of welfare state spending may even be 'self-financing' for the government – an example of virtuous welfare state dynamics. In countries with wide-ranging ('universal') welfare state arrangements, income mobility over the individual's life cycle also

I am grateful for research assistance by Christina Håkansson. Jordi Gual and Giuseppe Bertola have provided helpful comments on a previous version of this chapter.

39

seems to be relatively strong (Björklund and Jäntti, 1993). Moreover, it is often hypothesized that high income security contributes to tolerance of continuing reallocation of resources. We may also speculate that income security and poverty relief, up to a point, tend to boost social and political stability. Indeed, there is some empirical support for this speculation (Alesina and Rodrik, 1994).

What, then, are the main weaknesses of today's social arrangements in Europe? Hence, what are the basic arguments for welfare state reforms? In very general terms, it is useful to distinguish between three types of weaknesses.

First, the financial viability of some welfare state arrangements is not very robust to shocks, for instance, in demography, productivity growth, macroeconomic fluctuations and unemployment. Indeed, a combination of such disturbances is a basic explanation for recurring financial problems for the welfare state in recent decades. A main reason is that promised benefits are usually not contingent on the performance of the national economy and hence on the development of the aggregate tax base.

Second, the architects of European welfare states were not sufficiently attentive to the possibility of undesirable behavioural adjustments of individuals in response to welfare state arrangements and their financing. I refer, for instance, to the fact that tax wedges create deviations between social and private return to effort by favouring leisure, home production, barter of goods and services, and work in the shadow economy – not to mention tax avoidance and tax evasion. It is also a commonplace that taxes often distort decisions about saving and asset choice. Moreover, tax-induced disincentives of investment in human capital (in particular if taxes are progressive) counteract, or even reverse, the stimulation of such investment via education subsidies. These various consequences are, of course, the background for the common observation that social policies may conflict with efficient allocation of resources and high capacity utilization of factors of production, including labour. Indeed, it was an emerging understanding of these types of behaviour adjustment that helped initiate tax reforms in various countries in the late 1980s and early 1990s.

There is also an emerging understanding that welfare state arrangements are subject to 'moral hazard' and benefit cheating, i.e., induced behavioural changes that make new (and unintended) groups of individuals eligible for welfare state benefits. I will, however, also hypothesize that problems of moral hazard and benefit cheating have recently been accentuated by the erosion of social norms in favour of work, or against living on benefits – a process that may render the earlier mentioned virtuous circles *vicious* (Lindbeck, 1995).

Third, some socioeconomic conditions that existed when the present welfare states were built up have subsequently been transformed. I refer, in particular, to increased instability and heterogeneity of families, a rise in female labour force participation, higher unemployment, better-educated citizens with more individualistic values, tighter international economic integration and the emergence of new information and communication technology (ICT), with potentially important consequences for the organization of social insurance and social services. So far welfare state arrangements in Europe have only partially been adjusted to these developments.

When considering the possibility of mitigating these problems and limitations by reforms of various welfare state arrangements, the classical conflicts between insurance, incentives, administrative controls and distributional concerns are often difficult to avoid. It is then, however, also important to keep the earlier-mentioned achievements of the welfare state in mind to avoid derailing some of these.

Welfare state arrangements differ considerably among European countries. In general terms, these differences concern the relative role of the state, the family and the market for providing income security, redistribution and personal services. Countries also differ with respect to types of government intervention, such as the emphasis on universal benefits tied to citizenship (a typical feature of social arrangements in the Nordic countries), selective benefits to the poor (which are important in Anglo-Saxon countries) and occupational benefits tied to employment in different production sectors (arrangements that are particularly apparent in some countries on the European continent). Moreover, while social arrangements in continental European countries are usually strongly family-oriented, they are often tied more to individuals in the Nordic countries. The range of subsidized, or government-provided, household services also varies considerably among countries (here the Nordic governments spend the most).[1] I will, however, keep my discussion at a sufficiently general level to emphasize *common*

[1] Esping-Andersen (1990) was among the first to group countries into geographical and ideological clusters on the basis of such considerations.

welfare state achievements and problems in various West European countries, although differences among countries will also be pointed out. I organize the chapter as a 'journey' over the individual's life cycle from the cradle to the grave – from childhood, via working life (both when healthy and when sick), to the retirement period.

Childhood

Three types of welfare state arrangements seem to dominate with respect to childhood: health services for pregnant women and the newborn; child care during infancy; and schooling later on. There is hardly any controversy today about the proper role of the government concerning the first type of government intervention. We know that deficient health among pregnant women and small children tends to handicap the latter for life, and hence function as disinvestment in human capital – and that government subsidies and/or provision of health care for these groups alleviate such problems. The importance of government intervention is also quite non-controversial in the case of schooling. Although the main justification in the political arena is probably a combination of paternalism and distributional concern (including altruism), economists have also emphasized the difficulties for families of borrowing with expected future human capital as collateral and positive external effects of investment in human capital.

There is more controversy concerning the proper role of the government in the case of child care. One important reason for emerging interest in government financing and organization of child care is the gradual drop in nativity in most European countries. While a reproduction rate of 2.1 (the number of children per woman of reproduction age) is required for a constant population, abstracting from net migration, the rate in the EU today hovers around 1.5 per cent. Although, to begin with, fewer children reduce the economic burden for individuals of working age, it is well understood that the financial viability of government-financed pension systems and old-age care outside the family are threatened.

This, of course, is the background for proposals to boost nativity by redistributing income to families with children regardless of whether this is brought about via differentiation of taxes by number of children or via outright income transfers. However, in most countries it seems to have been easier for politicians to gain electoral support by transfers to the elderly than to families with small children, perhaps because voters in the latter group constitute a highly heterogeneous minority that is difficult to organize politically.

In addition to transfers to families with children ('child allowances'), some governments also encourage parenthood by tax-financed leave from work to take care of newborn children, 'parental leave' for short. In the Nordic countries, such leave is currently allowed for about a year. It is likely that such arrangements help explain why nativity is somewhat higher in these countries than on the European continent. A serious controversy, though, is whether it is a proper role of the government to influence deliberately the allocation of tasks within the family for the purpose of inducing males to devote more time to child care. Indeed, governments have taken this role in some countries, including Denmark and Sweden, by tying the rights to paid parental leave to the individual rather than to the family.

Another controversy concerns legislated rights of parents for tax-financed leave to take care of sick children. Again, a justification is to encourage parenthood. The system, however, is wide open to moral hazard and cheating. For instance, a recent study in Sweden concluded that about 10 per cent of parents who claimed such benefits on a specific day were, in fact, on the job and/or had their children at day-care centres rather than at home (RFV, 2002a).

There are also good reasons to provide economic support to single parents (usually mothers), not least to prevent child poverty. But the greater the generosity to this group, the more single mothers would be expected – via childbirth by unmarried women and divorce. Thus, it is unavoidable that such support functions as a subsidy on single parenthood – another example of moral hazard. It is also tempting for a parent to pretend to be single when, in fact, the individual lives with someone else. Administrative controls to counteract such tendencies are bound to create problems of personal integrity and hence to generate serious political resistance.

Are there, then, any arguments for additional government intervention in the field of child care? Yes, there is a ('second-best') efficiency argument for subsidizing child care *outside* the home to counteract the consequences of high marginal tax rates on labour earnings, which favour tax-free household work, including child care – at the expense of taxed work in the ordinary labour market and purchases of household services. In particular, subsidies for child care outside the family make it easier for females to combine labour force participation with parenthood. The Nordic countries have moved further in this direction than most other countries. This probably helps explain the relatively high labour force participation among females in these countries. Indeed, it is approximately the same, 70–75 per cent, as in the United States, where marginal tax rates are lower than in Europe and the relative prices of purchased child-care services are lower as a result of a wider dispersion of wages. Family policy in the rest of Europe still is rather closely tied to the 'male breadwinner' model, although labour force participation of married women has recently increased, typically to 45–55 per cent (outside the Nordic countries). This is an important example of limitations, or at least time lags, in the adjustment of social policy arrangements in view of changing socioeconomic conditions and individual preferences.

The differing levels of government involvement in the area of child care among European countries is reflected in statistics on government spending on formal day care. While such spending is between 1 and 2 per cent of GDP in Denmark, Sweden, Finland and Austria, it is below 0.5 per cent in other European countries, except in France where the figure is about 0.7 per cent (OECD, 2002, average for 1995–8).

In some Nordic countries (such as Sweden), however, the size of child-care subsidies outside the home is larger than necessary to compensate for the tax distortion – at least for families with more than one child. As a result, policy-induced distortions of the allocation of child care, and hence also of female labour force participation, have changed sign for families with more than one child. One conceivable explanation as to why such policies have been pursued may simply be that political decision-makers are not aware of the net incentive effect of government intervention in this field. Another explanation may be that politicians regard high female labour force participation as a goal in itself, a position often taken by feminist participants in the policy discussion. In the case of intellectually understimulated children, however, there is a specific (paternalistic) rationale for favouring child care outside, rather than inside, the family, namely the traditional 'head-start' argument. Indeed, there is empirical support for the asserted positive consequences for children of such head-start arrangements (Leibowitz, 1996).

A trivial policy conclusion in this context is that politicians have to consider carefully whether, and when, they want to favour child care within the family (as in most countries on the European continent) or outside the family (as in the Nordic countries in the case of families with more than one child) – or if they would prefer a neutral stance. The last option would clearly require *some* subsidies for child care outside the home in order to compensate for the general tax distortion in favour of household work. One unavoidable problem, though, is that taxes would then have to be higher than they would otherwise. Moreover, as often happens when we try to counteract one distortion by a new policy intervention, other distortions are created. In this specific case, the total volume of child care (by the family *and* others) would be favoured relative to the consumption of other goods and services (Rosen, 1997).

In many countries, there is increasing controversy in the case of both child care and schooling about whether the government should be neutral or partisan towards *alternative* providers of subsidized services. Observers anxious to 'homogenize' the future adult population in terms of types of knowledge and values tend to favour government-operated institutions. Those who emphasize freedom of choice instead tend to favour a neutral stance on the part of the government towards alternative providers, by allowing the subsidy to follow the child – the 'voucher method'. A general argument for more freedom of choice in this field is, of course, that competition, free entry and freedom to choose may boost economic efficiency and allow parents to satisfy individual preferences concerning methods of child care, teaching methods and, within certain bounds, types of curriculum. The gradually rising level of education among parents has also increased their demand for such freedom of choice, for the same reason as individuals demand more differentiated products in private markets when income rises. Although several countries today tend to move in the direction of increased freedom of choice for child care, the speed varies considerably. Somewhat surprisingly, school vouchers are more usual in 'collectivist' Sweden than, for instance, in the 'individualistic' United States.

The most common argument *against* freedom of choice in these areas seems to be a risk that children will be increasingly segregated in terms of their parents' education, profession and income. But in societies with considerable geographical segregation of housing, vouchers may instead contribute to desegregation of child care and schooling in these dimensions. Parents in poor neighbourhoods can use vouchers to enrol their children in preferred institutions, located in more affluent neighbourhoods with more highly educated parents. This probably explains why blacks in some parts of the United States have recently favoured voucher systems. In the case of child care, vouchers may alternatively be used to buy service at one of the parents' places of work. This may also contribute to desegregating children in terms of parents' education, profession and income, since the composition of the workforce within firms is often more varied socially than is the population across neighbourhoods. Freer choice is more likely to accentuate segregation in other dimensions, such as in terms of values and interests, in particular if religious institutions become important. So far, the lack of reliable empirical studies of the consequences in this respect makes it impossible to ascertain what the effects on segregation, or desegregation, actually are – or perhaps rather under what circumstances the effects go in one direction rather than the other.

Critics of parental choice in the case of child care and schooling have also asserted that the quality of government-operated institutions would suffer due to a tendency for talented children and personnel, in particular teachers, to move to private and co-operative institutions. A usual counterargument is that competition tends to improve the efficiency and quality of *all* institutions, partly by encouraging experimentation, partly by forcing low-quality public agencies out of business. Empirical research on this issue is in its infancy. But available studies have not provided support for the hypothesis that the quality of government-operated schools would suffer from more choice and competition – rather the opposite (Bergström and Sandström, 2001; Hepburn, 2001; Hoxby, 2002).

Employment and income security

In the case of healthy individuals, the most important welfare state interventions during an individual's working life are probably macroeconomic (monetary and fiscal) policies, minimum wages, job security legislation, unemployment benefits, active labour market policy and social assistance. The consequences of policies in these fields in Europe may be roughly summarized as good income security but poor employment performance.

The most obvious expression of the employment failure in Europe, of course, is the breakdown of full employment in the mid-1970s and early 1980s, and permanently high unemployment ever since. Typically, the open (official) unemployment rate has increased from 2–4 per cent in the 1960s and early 1970s to 8–12 per cent subsequently. There has been a related fall in the employment rate (for the population of working age) from about 70 to about 65 per cent. Although unemployment in Europe gradually fell during the boom in the late 1990s, there is still a long way to go before returning to pre-shock levels. Since 'full employment' has always been regarded as an important component, and indeed prerequisite, for a successful welfare state, its breakdown is certainly an important blow to the ambitions of social policies in Europe.

When trying to explain the poor employment performance in Europe, many observers have referred to an asserted rise in structural unemployment, or 'equilibrium unemployment', i.e., broadly speaking the level of unemployment that cannot be eliminated, except temporarily, by an expansion of aggregate demand. This assertion is often supported by reference to structural developments in the labour market, such as changes in the composition of the labour force, higher minimum wages, more generous unemployment benefits and stricter job security legislation that makes hiring more hazardous. It has, however, turned out to be difficult to identify changes in structural factors large enough and widespread enough among countries to explain such a huge asserted rise in the equilibrium unemployment rate. As an alternative, or at least a complement, we may regard the poor employment record in Europe in the past decade as a consequence of a *combination* of negative macroeconomic shocks and various mechanisms of unemployment persistence, i.e., mechanisms through which the (un)employment level moves only very slowly towards the pre-shock level (Lindbeck, 1996; Blanchard and Wolfers, 2000).

The origin of negative macroeconomic shocks hardly needs elaboration: the oil price hikes (in 1973 and 1979) and subsequent periods of highly restrictive economic policy to bring down inflation and budget deficits. Moreover, I agree with those who argue that there have been shifts in the composition of labour demand relative to supply in favour of highly skilled workers, although the evidence is indirect (anecdotal) rather than direct. But there has also been increased dispersion of wages and/or unemployment rates *within* narrowly defined subgroups of workers with quite similar occupations and statistically recorded skills. This observation is consistent with the (untested) hypothesis that the ongoing reorganization of firms has favoured individuals with certain *idiosyncratic* characteristics, in particular, high versatility and ability to take initiative and to co-operate with others in the production process (Lindbeck and Snower, 2000). In societies with rigid relative wages, demand shifts in favour of skilled workers and workers with specific personal characteristics are bound to create unemployment problems, thereby adding to the consequences of negative macroeconomic shocks. Except for the case of monopsony in the labour market (within a certain interval of wage rates), we would also expect that 'administrative' squeezes of the distribution of wages in the 1960s and 1970s have contributed to higher unemployment among workers with low expected productivity. This holds regardless of whether the administrative squeeze was brought about via higher minimum wages or via an egalitarian ('solidarity') wage policy by unions.

Against this background, it is natural to hypothesize that increased flexibility of relative wages would improve the employment performance for low-skilled workers, although a widening of the dispersion of wages may then be unavoidable. Since wages in the private sector are usually set by free bargaining, what the government can do in this sector is mainly opt for more relative wage flexibility in the public sector, be restrictive with minimum wage legislation and avoid legislation that makes collective bargaining agreements binding for non-organized workers.

A number of persistence mechanisms have also been identified in the literature (Lindbeck, 1996). When discussing the possibility of mitigating the consequences of such mechanisms, it is useful to distinguish between policies operating via the behaviour of labour market *outsiders*, i.e., individuals with unstable (or altogether without) jobs, and labour market *insiders*, i.e., workers with highly protected jobs.

In the case of outsiders, governments may mitigate unemployment persistence by either 'harsh' or 'lenient' policy measures. Examples of the former are less generous and stricter administration of unemployment benefits, possibly accompanied by shorter periods during which such benefits can be collected, and policies that keep the level of social assistance distinctly below the after-tax earnings of low-skilled workers. Suggestions regarding these types of policies, of course, illustrate the classical conflict between insurance, income distribution, incentives and administrative controls.

Subsidized, or even government-operated, retraining of low-skilled workers is perhaps the most celebrated example of 'lenient' methods to help outsiders get jobs. While such policies certainly keep down registered unemployment during training periods, there is hardly any convincing evidence that such policies improve the likelihood that the individual finds a regular job afterwards.[2] In terms of regular aggregate employment, the quantitative results of such policies have therefore been rather disappointing (Calmfors, Forslund and Hemström, 2001; Martin and Grubb, 2001).

While retraining is intended to move workers' productivity closer to existing, non-market-clearing wages, public works programmes and selective employment subsidies for low-skilled workers (such as so-called recruitment subsidies) instead try to mitigate the employment consequences of such wages. The latter types of programmes certainly provide jobs for individual workers. Empirical studies indicate, however, that regular jobs elsewhere are crowded out to a considerable extent, typically by about 50 per cent (Calmfors, Forslund and Hemström, 2001). Thus, again, the effects on aggregate employment are rather modest per euro spent; this seems to be the case, in particular, if the programmes are very large (covering several per cent of the labour force).

'In-work benefits', i.e., income supplements to the 'working poor', follow yet another track in the battle against persistent unemployment. In this case, low wages are combined with disposable earnings high enough to encourage labour supply and to make the 'working poor' somewhat less poor. This may be regarded as a *selective* negative income tax, reserved for low-income people who actually work. Although such arrangements avoid the disincentives for labour-force participation of a *general* negative income tax, they cannot prevent disincentives for hours of work and investment in human capital, in the latter case because the subsidy is reduced by higher wages. Thus, when employment subsidies or in-work benefits are raised, there is a case for a simultaneous increase in subsidies for education or training so as to counteract the disincentive effects on investment in human capital of

---

[2] By contrast, the experience of vocational training in the ordinary school system has been quite useful in keeping down youth unemployment, as illustrated by the experience in Austria, Germany and Switzerland, where youngsters are offered a combination of theoretical and vocational training in the form of apprentice systems. It is less clear to what extent such apprentice systems have kept down aggregate unemployment.

the former, although the budget cost for the government would then be raised.

One specific type of labour market policy, namely government-operated labour market exchange, or placement services, seems to have been more successful than other similar policies in mitigating unemployment persistence, provided such services are highly active and combined with strict administration of the unemployment benefit system (Martin and Grubb, 2001, and references therein). As in the case of training programmes, success, of course, presupposes that there are vacancies in the national economy, hence that aggregate demand on domestic output is sufficiently high.

An alternative, or perhaps rather a complement, to interventions designed to influence the behaviour of labour market outsiders consists of measures to reduce the market powers of *insiders*, i.e., workers with stable jobs, protected by labour market legislation and unions. I refer, for instance, to lower legislated costs of firing, and hence indirectly also lower costs of hiring workers. Since such costs tend to stabilize employment at whatever level it happens to be, the consequences for aggregate employment are positive if unemployment happens to be low initially, but detrimental if it happens to be high. As often pointed out in the literature, the effects of such costs on the *average* level of unemployment over the business cycle are uncertain. But the more the insiders exploit such legislation to boost real wages, the more likely it is that the average level of unemployment is reduced over the business cycle. This, then, is another illustration of the necessity of making a tradeoff between insurance and incentives, in this case as a result of a conflict of interest between insiders and outsiders in the labour market.

Many observers have also referred to rigidities in product markets – both as a result of taxes and government regulations, and as a consequence of spontaneous obstacles within the private sector. To the extent that such rigidities reduce competition in product markets, the labour demand curve will shift inward and become less elastic, both for individual firms and for the aggregate of firms (Layard, Nickel and Jackman, 1991; Nicoletti *et al.*, 2001). As a result, aggregate labour demand tends to fall. Moreover, various government restrictions on the entry of firms means that the supply response to increased aggregate product demand is constrained, which would also be expected to contribute to unemployment persistence. Nicoletti *et al.* (2001) conclude that combinations of rigidities in product and labour markets, which are common, tend to be particularly harmful for the performance of the labour market.

It is also tempting to hypothesize that rigidities in capital markets reduce the output and employment response to positive shocks in aggregate demand, and hence contribute to unemployment persistence. Obvious examples are the difficulties for small and medium-sized firms in obtaining capital, for instance, because banks are heavily involved with established firms. Thus, to improve the employment situation in European countries, reforms in capital markets are also likely to be helpful.

It is true that a great number of minor ad hoc changes in labour-, product- and capital-market legislation have been carried out during the last decades, but different policy measures have often worked in different directions in terms of the effects on unemployment persistence. According to available studies (for instance, Bertola *et al.*, 2001, and Nicoletti *et al.*, 2001), it is doubtful whether the *sum* of all changes in rules and regulations in labour, product and capital markets implemented so far have actually facilitated a return to full employment (Bertola *et al.*, 2001) – except for in a few countries such as the Netherlands and perhaps the UK.

We may also hypothesize that long periods of unemployment weaken social norms in favour of work, or against living on various types of benefits. As a result, 'unemployment cultures' may emerge (Lindbeck, 1996). If this (also untested) hypothesis makes sense, here is an additional persistence mechanism, and a further argument as to why governments should try hard *both* to counteract large negative macroeconomic shocks (mainly by aggregate demand management) *and* to fight persistence mechanisms.

As a result of the stalemate in the areas of structural reforms in many countries, the insider–outsider divide in the labour market has continued. An insider–outsider divide, however, also exists in other areas. An example is the provision of social benefits, such as unemployment benefits, sick pay and occupational pensions, which often are tied to regular work, which means that labour market outsiders do not benefit much. Another example is rent control, which has created a strong insider–outsider division in the housing markets in many cities. When an individual is an outsider in all these markets – the labour market, the housing market and social benefits – so-called 'social exclusion' is unavoidable. Obvious examples of groups in this situation are school dropouts, some immigrant groups, drug and alcohol addicts, individuals with physical and mental handicaps and so forth.

Why then are the political systems in Europe so limited in their ability to undertake institutional reform for the purpose of mitigating persistent unemployment? One explanation may simply be that neither politicians nor the electorate – not even all economists – are convinced that policy measures of the types discussed above would be of much help in reducing persistently high unemployment. If so, then, in my view, it would be difficult to understand why Europe has serious long-lasting employment problems in the first place. It is also likely that powerful interest groups – labour unions, incumbent production firms and incumbent financial institutions – have blocked many potentially useful measures.

Sick-leave insurance and health care

Important arguments for government intervention in the fields of sick leave and health care are that some individuals are myopic (a paternalistic argument) and that some tend to free ride on the altruism of others (they assume that someone will help them if they are too sick to work or need health care in the future). There is also an income distribution argument for government intervention, since low-income groups often cannot afford voluntary insurance policies. The economics literature also emphasizes deficiencies in the markets for health insurance due to asymmetric information between insurance providers and individuals who seek insurance. As a result, health insurance becomes expensive and the market for health insurance will be thin – either because of 'adverse selection' (when the insurance provider cannot judge the health status of individuals), or because of 'cream skimming' (when insurance companies have the ability to select low-risk individuals as customers). In most developed countries, the political response to these problems has been mandatory sick-leave insurance and government-subsidized or -provided health care.

It is, however, well known that government interventions in these fields encounter serious problems today. In the case of sick-leave insurance, moral hazard is difficult to avoid. After all, individuals have considerable discretion in deciding whether they are in sufficiently good shape to go to work or not. Although the prevalence of moral hazard is difficult to prove rigorously, there are indicators that it actually is a problem. For instance, it is difficult to explain differences in sick absentees among countries by differences in health indicators (Kangas, 1991); health statistics may not, however, correctly reflect the actual health status of the population. Another indicator is that varying requirements concerning doctors' certification of sickness, and the strength of administrative controls, help explain the incidence of sick absentees among countries (*ibid.*). Moreover, a tighter labour market tends to increase the number of sick absentees. Empirical studies suggest that this phenomenon not only reflects a statistical 'selection effect', when more people with health problems become employed in business upswings. It is also likely that it is less risky for an employee to stay at home when the labour market is tight (Arai and Skogman Thoursie, 2001; Askildsen, Bratberg and Nilsen, 2002). One piece of evidence supporting this interpretation is that people with temporary job contracts have fewer sick days than people with permanent job contracts (Arai and Skogman Thoursie, 2001; Ichino and Riphahn, 2002).

But how, then, do we explain the *rising trend* in sick absenteeism in recent decades in some countries? Until recently, a stepwise increase in the generosity of benefit rules may have been a fitting explanation, since sick absenteeism seems to increase with the generosity of benefit levels (Barmby, Sessions and Treble, 1994; Henrekson, Lantto and Persson, 1994; Johansson and Palme, 2001). More recent increases in sick absenteeism, however, have often taken place during periods of unchanged rules. How, then, do we explain this?

The gradual ageing of the population is one obvious explanation. But more complex forces seem to be at work. A quite popular hypothesis is that sick leave has risen due to a deterioration of so-called mental working conditions, including more stress at work. If this hypothesis actually made sense, an obvious policy measure would be experience-rated insurance fees, i.e., higher fees not only for firms with many work injuries but also for firms with high sick absenteeism for other reasons. But is this hypothesis really consistent with the observation that numbers of sick absentees have increased only in *some* countries, mainly the Netherlands, Norway and Sweden?

The remedy would be more complex if the rise in sick absentees could be attributed to developments within the family, for instance, scarcity of time in connection with greater female labour force participation.

Since women are still more responsible for household work than men (according to time budgets), this explanation would be consistent with the observation that females account for considerably higher sick absence than men. It is also suggestive that sick absenteeism among women has increased, in particular, in countries with high female labour force participation and generous insurance rules (RFV, 2002b: 11).

If this possible explanation for increased numbers of sick absentees makes sense, one remedy might be to make it easier for households to obtain services from outside. For instance, suppose that the marginal tax rate is 50 per cent for both the buyer and the seller of household services (such as caretakers of children, craftsmen or gardeners). The buyer has to earn four times as much before tax as the seller gets after tax in order to finance the purchase of additional services in the market. It is easy to understand that households choose to produce services themselves in such societies, and that this helps explain the scarcity of time within families in which both spouses participate in the labour market. If it turns out to be impossible to mitigate this problem by lower marginal tax rates, an obvious alternative is subsidies for the purchase of certain household services in the market, or even government provision of some such services. Indeed, such policy measures have recently been implemented in Belgium and France. It is unavoidable, however, that new distortions would then emerge, since all types of household services that are close substitutes to the household's own production can hardly be subsidized; moreover, even higher taxes would now be necessary.

There may, however, be more complex explanations for the rise in sick absentees in countries with generous sick-leave benefits. Social norms in favour of work, or against living on sick-leave benefits, may have receded over time – in a similar fashion as 'unemployment cultures' seem to have developed in some geographical areas. In this way, moral hazard would have been accentuated by a gradually more 'liberal' interpretation by the individual himself of the rules of sickness absenteeism. For instance, suppose that the number of individuals with sick pay has increased as a result of more generous benefits or a reduced risk of losing one's job because of lower aggregate unemployment. Individuals would then be likely to feel less guilt (or shame) to call in sick when, in fact, they are able to work (for a general discussion of such mechanisms, see Lindbeck, Nyberg and Weibull (1999)).

Social norms against plain *cheating* on sick-leave benefits may also have weakened among certain groups. For instance, recent opinion polls suggest that a majority of the adult population in Sweden believes that it is all right to stay home with paid sick leave without being sick – for instance, when a woman is pregnant, when an individual takes care of relatives or simply when someone feels miserable at the thought of having to go to work (RFV, 2002a). Another indicator of cheating on sick leave is that a significant number of males call in sick when important sports events are shown on television (Skogman Thoursie, 2002).

Another example of either moral hazard or benefit cheating is that individuals move between different benefit systems in response to changes in relative benefit levels. This is exactly what happened in Sweden in the 1980s, when the benefit level in the work-injury system was raised above the level in the sick-pay system, with the result that some individuals shifted from sick benefits to work-injury benefits. Metaphorically, people suddenly discovered that their backache had been caused by injury at work rather than by sitting around watching television at home. A study in Sweden also suggests that the rules of unemployment benefits influence the propensity to live on sick pay (Larsson, 2002). It is also striking that sick leave is particularly high in regions with high unemployment in Sweden. Since there is hardly any evidence that this can be explained by geographical variations in health conditions, it is likely that some individuals simply choose sick benefits rather than (less generous) unemployment benefits. Thus, there is a case for having the same benefit level in all benefit schemes among which individuals can move freely at their own discretion, for instance, between sick-pay insurance, work-injury insurance, unemployment benefits and early retirement.

There is still not enough reliable empirical research to make us confident about how to reduce the incidence of sick absenteeism. There is, however, probably a case for a broad approach, relying on many different measures. Incentives for firms to improve the work environment via experience-rated sick-insurance fees and measures that reduce time stress among family members are very general policies for this purpose. When changes in the rules of sick-pay insurance are considered, there is an obvious tradeoff between stronger incentives, tighter administrative controls and more active 'rehabilitation' measures, designed to help individuals return to work. Stronger incentives include more waiting days (days without sick pay) and more co-insurance, i.e., lower benefit levels. Tighter administrative controls include stricter requirements for doctor's certificates and visits by administrators in the individual's home. Useful rehabilitation may require tight co-operation among health-insurance providers, health-care institutions and employers.

So much for sick-leave insurance. Problems connected with *health care* are also quite complex. In general terms, a basic problem is how tax financing or insurance should be combined with economic efficiency. For instance, countries with mandatory health-care insurance, such as Germany, often find it quite difficult to control costs, which is a general problem when a 'third party pays'. (The same problem arises in voluntary health-insurance programmes, for instance, in the United States.) Countries with tax-financed health care, like the UK, have often been more successful at putting a lid on costs by implementing strict budget limits. But this creates serious problems of access, reflected in queues and long waiting times, as well as complaints about poor quality of services. The standard suggestion for shortening such queues is to expand the resources that are available for health care. But then it has to be specified whether this should be achieved via cuts in other spending programmes or via higher taxes.

There is also a more fundamental objection to simply pouring additional resources into health care. Research indicates that health conditions in rich countries today are more highly related to life style than to the volume of health care provided (Fuchs, 1986). From this point of view, policies that induce individuals to choose a healthier life style sound like an ideal solution to the problem of galloping costs in the health-care sector. The question is how this could conceivably be brought about. Although government-provided, or -subsidized, information about health hazards is now generally accepted in the case of smoking and drugs, it is difficult to determine how far the government can stretch its life-style advice without being regarded as excessively paternalistic. Direct government intervention by means of incentives and regulations is another option. Such intervention is generally accepted in the case of taxes on cigarettes and alcohol as well as in the case of compulsory use of seat belts. But would the general public also condone high taxes on fatty foods and laws prescribing helmets for cyclists? It may be tempting for a government to argue that overweight people and cyclists without helmets create negative external effects on the government-subsidized health-care system and hence on the taxpayer. There would then be a rather short step to recommending that the government intervene by using taxes, subsidies or regulations to change people's behaviour – even though the government itself, albeit for good reasons, has created the externality (via mandatory, collectively financed health care).

Another important consideration in connection with government-operated health care is the issue of individual freedom of choice. Here a well-known difficulty with allowing free choice is that information about diagnosis and treatment of health problems is highly asymmetric between patients and health providers. As a result, it is often argued that freedom of choice would not be of much value in this area. But with a gradually better-educated population, and with so much health information on the web, this asymmetry is likely to diminish considerably over time (Lindbeck and Wikström, 2000). There are strong incentives to use the new information and communication system (ICT, including the Internet) to acquire knowledge about a particular disease, without having to be knowledgeable about medicine in general. This will probably boost the demand for freedom to choose a health clinic, hospital, physician, nurse, etc. This in turn raises the question of *how* such freedom of choice should be organized. Distributing vouchers with the same value to individuals is certainly not a very useful device in this case because of the heterogeneity of health-care needs. But within the framework of either health-care insurance or tax-financed health care, it is certainly possible to allow considerably more freedom of choice than at present in most countries. Public-sector administrators in the health-care sector may also outsource health-care services to different (public and private) producers among which individuals are allowed to choose.

My trivial conclusion is that there is a case for encouraging experimentation in health care even when the government basically finances it. This obviously requires considerable freedom of entry for non-governmental service providers – health clinics, hospitals and self-employed physicians and nurses. Examples of such experimentation include occupation-related health care, health clubs and health maintenance organizations (HMOs), private health-care centres and hospitals (including hospitals run by foundations). Such experimentation would most likely result in a *network* of public and private health providers. Complex problems of supervision and regulation may, of course, arise along with the entry of many types of health-care providers, not unlike such problems in privatized industries, such as electricity and telecommunications. It would therefore be a good idea to build up rather elaborate systems of supervision and regulation in conjunction with experimentation and increased freedom of entry.

Pensions and old-age care

The justification for government provision of pension annuities is rather similar to the justification for mandatory unemployment benefits and mandatory sick-leave and health-care insurance: to counteract the consequences of myopic behaviour, free riding and deficiencies in voluntary insurance markets.

Politicians have, however, also been eager to use mandatory pension systems as tools of income redistribution. In the case of pay-as-you-go (or simply 'paygo') pension systems, politicians, then, have been particularly generous to the first generations of paygo pensioners, who often received pensions with a capital value five or ten times the capital value of their own contributions to the pension system. Of course, this gift has to be paid for by subsequent generations; indeed, it can be shown that the present value of the gift to the first generation is of the same size as the capital value of the loss for subsequent generations (Lindbeck and Persson, 2003 forthcoming).

What, then, are the main problems inherent in contemporary paygo pension systems in European countries? When individuals have been promised certain pension benefits, which is the case in so-called defined benefit (DB) systems, there is a lack of financial viability in the event of unexpected stagnation of the tax bases, for instance, as a result of changes in demography and productivity growth. There may also be unintended behavioural adjustments among individuals in response to the pension system itself. For instance, government provision of pensions is likely to have contributed to the earlier discussed fall in nativity, since such arrangements make it less necessary for couples to have children of their own to support them in old age. Moreover, generous conditions for early retirement help explain the fall in the de facto retirement age, which is about fifty-seven today in Europe. Mandatory pension arrangements also create disincentives for work during active years because of the implicit marginal tax wage in paygo pension systems, since the return is usually lower than market interest rates. Paygo pension systems often also reduce saving and hence the capital stock in particular as a result of the 'gift' to the first generation of paygo pensioners.

Owing to these problems, various types of pension reforms have recently been discussed, and to some extent already implemented. Three types of reforms have predominated: (a) marginal reforms of existing paygo systems; (b) shifts to contribution-based, i.e., defined contribution (DC) systems, with individual accounts, still of the paygo type (often denoted 'notional defined contribution', or NDC systems); and (c) partial or total shifts to actuarially fair, fully funded systems.

(a) So far, *marginal reforms* have dominated, mainly as a response to recent threats to the financial viability of existing paygo systems. These reforms have been characterized by ad hoc increases in contribution rates and/or cuts in pension benefits (possibly in the form of modification of price indices). Often the actual implementation of reforms has been postponed quite far into the future (McHale, 1999) to avoid sudden, unexpected deterioration of pension entitlements. But a problem with such postponements is that they may be followed by additional postponements later on.

If the threat to the future financial viability of a pension system arises due to falling birth rates, obvious remedies are attempts to boost either nativity or the immigration of young workers – although the political realism of the latter option may be limited by fears of ethnic conflict in future. If the financial problems are instead a result of greater longevity after retirement, a natural remedy is to increase the statutory pension age and remove subsidies for early retirement. After all, increased longevity is presumably correlated with a greater capacity to work in old age. Several countries have also closed a number of 'pathways' to early retirement outside the ordinary pension system, not only by stricter rules for receiving disability pensions, but also by reducing the possibilities for elderly, unemployed workers to receive long-term sick leave or early retirement.

Ad hoc adjustments often take time to be agreed and implemented, which means that serious financial problems for the pension system may emerge in the meantime. Unpredictable ad hoc adjustments also create uncertainty for individuals regarding the future rules of the game. Both problems may be mitigated to some extent by introducing automatic adjustment mechanisms in the pension system, i.e., strict rules for how pension benefits or contributions should be adjusted to various types of shocks. For instance, rules may be established about the extent to which benefits and contributions should be automatically adjusted in response to specified changes in expected longevity after the statutory retirement age, or in response to expected deficits in the pension system. For instance, per capita pension benefits may be adjusted downward in proportion to a recorded rise in expected longevity of pensioners. Or contributions may be adjusted upward to balance the pension budget.

(b) A number of countries, including Italy, the Netherlands, Lithuania and Sweden, have recently carried more radical reforms of their paygo pension systems by shifting to NDC systems. Broadly speaking, the pension benefit of an individual in such a system is proportional to his accumulated lifetime pension contributions. In order for such a system to become financially viable, the proportionality factor and hence the return on mandatory pension saving have to be tied to the growth rate of the tax base of the economy. Since this growth rate is usually smaller than the return in financial markets, an NDC system may therefore be described as 'quasi-actuarial' in contrast to an 'actuarially fair', fully funded system, where the return is determined by conditions in financial markets.

A main advantage of shifting to a quasi-actuarial system is that the implicit marginal tax wedge would be reduced because of a tighter link between an individual's contributions and his subsequent pension benefits. (Some steps in this direction could also be taken in earnings-based pension systems by tying pension benefits to lifetime earnings rather than to earnings during only the individual's last x years or y best years.) With realistic assumptions, the tax wedge would be cut approximately in half when moving from a completely non-actuarial to a quasi-actuarial system – often from about 20 to about 10 per cent (Lindbeck and Persson, 2003 forthcoming). Such a reform also implies that existing subsidies for early retirement would basically be removed. It would then also be relatively easy to allow individuals free choice of retirement age.

To avoid situations in which the removal of incentives to retire early results in high unemployment for elderly workers, it is, of course, also important to increase opportunities for elderly workers to get jobs. Otherwise, they may simply be shifted from the pension system to other benefit systems, e.g., unemployment insurance, sick leave, disability pensions or social assistance. This is an additional argument for labour market reforms to bring about increased flexibility of both working hours and wages – at least for the elderly.

(c) There is also a recent trend to more funding of pension systems. A main argument for a *total* shift to such a system is that the return on the mandatory pension system would then coincide with the return in financial markets, and hence that the implicit tax wedge would be removed. It should be kept in mind that this gain materializes only for future generations, after the pension claims of the old paygo pensioners have been paid and financed by taxes on some transitional generations. By such 'front-loading', a shift to funded pension systems would also boost the aggregate saving rate of the national economy. This, of course, is tantamount to suggesting that a pension reform should be used as a tool for changing the distribution of income in favour of future generations. Technically speaking, such a rise in aggregate saving and investment rates does not require a pension reform. A rise in aggregate saving could alternatively be brought about by a higher government budget surplus or increased incentives for private saving. Proposals, then, to use pension reform to raise aggregate national saving seem to reflect attempted 'framing' to make it politically easier to achieve national goals for aggregate saving.

There is a stronger case for a *partial* than for a total shift to a funded, actuarially fair pension system. Indeed, some countries have recently started to move in this direction, or are at least contemplating such a move. A main advantage would be that people could then enjoy a more diversified portfolio of pension claims than in *either* a pure paygo system, in which the risky return is connected to the growth rate of the tax base, *or* a fully funded system in which the risky return depends on developments in financial markets. The diversification effect would be particularly strong if the portfolios of the funded system included a large fraction of foreign assets. In other words, by having some pension claims based on the return on foreign assets, a pensioner would be less dependent than in a paygo system on what happens to the national economy in his own country.

The 'political risks' probably also differ between paygo and funded pension claims. This is an additional argument for combining paygo and funded systems. A usual assessment is that the risks of political interventions in pension entitlements are smaller if they are funded, since such a system may 'borrow' property rights from private pension contracts – another illustration of 'framing'. Government-operated funded systems are, however, connected with risks other than those of private pension funds. In particular, government-operated pension funds may lead to an irresistible temptation for politicians to intervene in the management of fund assets. There is also a risk that politicians, or their representatives, will be appointed to the boards of firms in which the fund owns shares. As a result, large pension funds in mandatory government-controlled pension systems may result in a highly politicized national economy – in fact, rather similar to a highly nationalized economy. It is much easier for power-prone politicians to seize powers over existing, government-initiated pension funds than to pursue outright nationalization of firms 'from scratch'. To reduce such risks, it is crucial that the funds are privately managed from the outset, and that the individual is allowed to choose the fund manager.

Another concern is whether we want the pension system to function as a device for income redistribution and risk sharing *within* generations. Existing paygo systems often do so to some extent. Such redistribution and risk sharing tend to disappear with a shift *either* to a quasi-actuarial paygo system (with a strong link between contributions and benefits) *or* to an actuarially fair, fully funded pension system. If such risk sharing is regarded as a desirable feature of a pension system, then it serves as another illustration of the conflict between insurance and incentives. It is, however, technically possible to construct tools other than pension arrangements to bring about redistribution and risk sharing among and within generations. Obvious examples are fiscal policy devices such as intergenerational government debt policies and progressive taxation.

Existing paygo pension systems also create income sharing and income insurance *within families*, in particular by protecting widows and their children. One way to provide such protection, also within quasi-actuarial and actuarially fair pension systems, is simply to assign a spouse legal property rights to the other spouse's pension claims in the reformed system. This would also protect spouses in the event of divorce. Should the same rules apply in the case of cohabitation?

The slowdown in productivity growth in Europe during recent decades and the ageing of the population create serious financial problems not only for government-operated pension systems, but also for *old-age care*. Moreover, this sector has been hard hit by 'Baumol's Law', according to which the relative costs of labour-intensive services gradually increase because of slower productivity growth than in manufacturing. After all, old-age care consists mainly of personal care that is difficult to rationalize to any large extent.

The choice between insurance and tax financing is associated more or less with the same problems as health care in general. But the possibilities of allowing freedom of choice, for instance via voucher systems, are much greater. This holds, in particular, for simple household services for the elderly in their homes – shopping, cooking, cleaning, companionship etc. When medical requirements are modest, vouchers may also be useful in the case of institutionalized old-age care. Still, as in the case of medical care in general, greater freedom of choice than today is certainly also feasible in the case of more intensive medical services. But since elderly patients have substantial difficulties in making themselves heard, there is a particularly strong case for supervision of services provided. Presumably, these needs increase if entry of service providers is opened up.

Concluding remarks

Social policies, and hence welfare state arrangements, may to a large extent be seen as rational responses to market failures, myopic or free-riding behaviour of individuals and redistributional ambitions (based on self-interest as well as altruism) of the general public. But such arrangements also suffer from a number of limitations and weaknesses, such as (a) financial instability in response to shocks; (b) undesirable behavioural adjustments in response to the arrangements themselves; and (c) only limited adjustments of these arrangements to contemporary changes in socioeconomic conditions. Entrenched special interests and complications in party politics have, however, made it difficult to remove these deficiencies.

So far, financial instability has mainly been dealt with by marginal, ad hoc modifications of existing welfare state arrangements. Indeed, such adjustments will always be necessary. It may also be useful, however, to incorporate automatic adjustment mechanisms into certain social arrangements to bring about faster, and perhaps also less politically controversial, adjustments. So far, such reforms have been introduced mainly in pension systems, often in the context of shifts from defined benefit (DB) to defined contribution (DC) systems. In some countries, such reforms have taken the form of shifts to fully funded, actuarially fair systems, in other countries of transformations of existing paygo systems to so-called notional defined contribution (NDC) systems, which I earlier characterized as 'quasi-actuarial'.

Undesirable behavioural adjustments have been particularly observed in the labour market. This has, for instance, been reflected in difficulties in reconciling job protection for insiders with good employment prospects for low-skilled workers. Schematically speaking, the United Kingdom (like the United States) has emphasized the latter aspect, at the expense of job protection and distributional concerns – although such concerns have been taken into account to some extent by 'in-work benefits' to the working poor. Countries on the European continent have instead emphasized job protection, at the expense of a pronounced insider–outsider divide in the labour market. Southern Europe may be characterized broadly in the same way, although with more low-skilled jobs in informal sectors, and with more intergenerational income sharing within families. The Nordic countries differ from countries on the continent mainly by greater government provision of household services, in particular, in the case of child care and old-age care, which has contributed to high female labour force participation. Indeed, with the high tax burden that prevails in these countries, it is financially hazardous to have one spouse stay at home to take care of children.

In all European countries, it has turned out to be particularly difficult to deal with moral hazard and benefit cheating – for instance, in the case of unemployment benefits, the support of single mothers, sick-leave insurance and early retirement for asserted health reasons. Such problems are bound to be particularly serious if social norms in favour of work, and hence against living on benefits, recede over time when the number of beneficiaries increases, for instance, as a result of smaller economic incentives to work or a rise in the number of beneficiaries after unemployment-creating macroeconomic shocks. This implies that the welfare state may wind up in a vicious circle if weaker economic incentives to work gradually make living on benefits more socially acceptable. To finance the higher costs of welfare state arrangements, politicians may have to raise taxes further, which makes work even less rewarding as compared to living on benefits, with even smaller incentives for work and possibly also a further weakening of work norms etc.

The welfare state has basically been a *national* project. How, then, will increased international economic integration affect the European social models? Some observers have predicted a 'race to the bottom' of both the social assistance level and the redistributional ambitions of the tax system. So far, however, there is not much evidence of such a race (Bertola *et al.*, 2001). It could, of course, become a serious problem in the future, for instance, if national labour markets become much more internationally integrated than today, so that low-skilled individuals move to countries with relatively strong income protection and redistributional ambitions, while highly skilled individuals move in the opposite direction. Clearly, such tendencies are likely to be accentuated in connection with the geographical enlargement of the EU to countries with relatively low per capita income.

A common minimum level of social assistance for all countries may not be a feasible solution to this problem as long as average income differs dramatically between the countries in the western and eastern parts of the future EU. An alternative, discussed by Sinn (2000), would be to opt for different social assistance levels within a nation, depending on the country of origin of the individual. But would such a set-up be politically feasible?

The policies that are most likely to encounter a 'race to the bottom' are corporate taxes and individual capital income taxes. We may perhaps also expect taxes on personal income and consumer goods to converge. When looking at this issue, it is, however, important to consider the entire 'package' of benefits and taxes for highly taxed groups, rather than their marginal tax rates alone. Moreover, experience from the United States indicates that such tax rates may differ by several percentage points among neighbouring states without serious problems. For obvious reasons, larger differences than within the United States may certainly survive within Europe.

Clearly, increased mobility of labour also raises the issue of the transferability of entitlements – in principle, in a similar way as the transferability of occupational pensions among firms and industries within countries. Presumably, this problem is easier to solve in the case of contribution-based systems with individual accounts than in benefit-based systems (without such accounts). It would, therefore, seem that the internationalization process favours quasi-actuarial and actuarially fair systems with individual accounts, as compared to traditional defined benefit systems.

International complications may also arise in the case of tax-financed social services. Will the government in nation A be willing to pay for its citizens' health care in country B? If so, one possibility would be international agreements about the rights of the authorities in country

B to bill the authorities in country A, and vice versa, with clearing mechanisms among national governments. Indeed, it is not unlikely that the legal authorities of the EU will grant individuals in member countries the right to receive social services in all EU countries, with a legislated duty of the individual's home country to pay.

Standardization of welfare state arrangements in different countries is sometimes suggested as a method of dealing with international complications such as these. But there are also good reasons to avoid this route. It would seem that welfare state arrangements often function best when they are anchored in domestic traditions and social and political structures. Another reason is that standardization would make decentralized experimentation more difficult. There is also value in the possibility for individuals to choose in which 'policy regime' to live, including welfare state arrangements and taxes. Voting with one's feet is an important complement to voting at the ballot box.

Moreover, the explosive development of information and communication technology, ICT, is likely to contribute to better-informed decisions than in earlier generations (Lindbeck and Wikström, 2002); the number of sites on the Internet where such information is provided is growing rapidly. ICT has also potentially important consequences for the administration of national and international welfare state arrangements. For instance, international clearing mechanisms for the payment of social security benefits and the financing of social services can be simplified.

ICT also lowers the costs of operating systems with individual accounts, which favours quasi-actuarial and actuarially fair pension systems as compared to traditional defined benefit systems. ICT also opens up new channels for citizens to influence types and quality of public sector services. The ordinary political process, i.e., the ballot box, is a blunt method for influencing types and quality of services provided by specific public sector institutions, such as a certain school or a childcare centre. The reason, of course, is that electoral campaigns deal with packages of policy issues, often dominated by national politics. ICT offers new ways for citizens not only to acquire better information from public sector agencies but also to communicate interactively with specific public sector service institutions, including providers of social services. In fact, in some cases, ICT has great potential for *delivering* services via the Internet; important examples are education and health care.

In particular, ICT strengthens an individual citizen's 'voice', when many people simultaneously express their views via the Internet. This development is especially important in the public sector, since the exit option is so weak. Of course, the voice option would become much more powerful if there were also exit opportunities in the form of alternative suppliers, for instance, via voucher systems. There is no reason to assume that exit opportunities, and hence freedom of choice and competition, are less important and useful in the case of social services than in the case of other products.

So my simple bottom line is that there is a huge need, and vast possibilities, to improve the performance of European social models – in terms of employment, benefit programmes and social services. The question is whether politicians are willing and able to grasp these opportunities, which often requires both courage and skill in coalition building.

References

Alesina, A. and D. Rodrik (1994), 'Distributive politics and economic growth', *Quarterly Journal of Economics*, 109 (May): 465–490.

Arai, M. and P. Skogman Thoursie (2001), 'Incentives and selection in cyclical absenteeism', FIEF Working Paper Series No. 167, Stockholm: Labour Union Institute for Economic Research.

Askildsen, J. E., E. Bratberg and O. A. Nilsen (2002), 'Unemployment, labor force composition and sickness absence: a panel data study', IZA Discussion Paper No. 446, Bonn: Institute for the Study of Labor.

Barmby, T. A., J. Sessions and J. G. Treble (1994), 'Absenteeism, efficiency wages and shirking', *Scandinavian Journal of Economics*, 96: 561–566.

Bergström, F. and F. M. Sandström (2001), 'Competition and the quality of public schools' (mimeo), Swedish Research Institute of Trade, Stockholm.

Bertola, G., J. F. Jimeno, R. Marimon and C. Pissarides (2001), 'EU welfare systems and labor markets: diverse in the past, integrated in the future?', in G. Bertola, T. Boeri and G. Nicoletti, *Welfare and unemployment in a united Europe*, Cambridge, MA: MIT Press, pp. 23–122.

Björklund, A. and M. Jäntti (1993), 'Intergenerational income mobility in Sweden compared to the United States' (mimeo), Institute for Social Research (SOFI), Stockholm University.

Blanchard, O. and J. Wolfers (2000), 'The role of shocks and institutions in the rise in European unemployment: the aggregate evidence', *Economic Journal*, 110: 1–33.

Calmfors, L., A. Forslund and M. Hemström (2001), 'Does active labour market policy work? Lessons from the Swedish experiences', *Swedish Economic Policy Review*, 8(2): 61–124.

Esping-Andersen, G. (1990), *The three worlds of welfare capitalism*, Oxford: Oxford University Press.

Fuchs, V. R. (1986), *The health economy*, Cambridge, MA: Harvard University Press.

Henrekson, M., K. Lantto and M. Persson (1994), *Bruk och missbruk av sjukförsäkringen* [Use and misuse of health insurance], Stockholm: SNS Förlag.

Hepburn, C. R. (2001), *Can the market save our schools?*, Vancouver: Fraser Institute.

Hoxby, C. (2002), 'School choice and school productivity', NBER Working Paper No. 8873, Cambridge, MA: National Bureau of Economic Research.

Ichino, A. and R. T. Riphahn (2002), 'The effects of employment protection on worker effort: a comparison of absenteeism during and after probation', CESifo Working Paper No. 596, Munich: CESifo.

Johansson, P. and M. Palme (2001), 'Assessing the effects of public policy on worker absenteeism', *Journal of Human Resources*, 37(2): 381–405.

Kangas, O. (1991), 'Behov eller rättighet? Sjukfrånvarons strukturella och institutionella bestämningsfaktorer i OECD-länderna' [Need or right? Structural and institutional determinants of sick absenteeism in OECD countries], *Sociologisk Forskning*, 3: 23–41.

Larsson, L. (2002), 'Sick of being unemployed? Interactions between unemployment and sickness insurance in Sweden', IFAU Working Paper Series 2002:6, Uppsala: Institute for Labor Market Policy Evaluation.

Layard, R. S., N. Nickel and R. Jackman (1991), *Unemployment: macroeconomic performance and the labor market*, Oxford: Oxford University Press.

Leibowitz, A. (1996), 'Child care: private costs or public responsibility?', in V. Fuchs (ed.), *Individual and social responsibility*, Chicago: University of Chicago Press, ch. 2.

Lindbeck, A. (1995), 'Hazardous welfare-state dynamics', *American Economic Review*, Papers and Proceedings, 85: 9–15.

(1996), 'The West European employment problem', *Weltwirtschaftliches Archiv*, 132 (4) (December): 3–31.

Lindbeck, A., S. Nyberg and J. W. Weibull (1999), 'Social norms and economic incentives in the welfare state', *Quarterly Journal of Economics*, 114: 1–35.

Lindbeck, A. and M. Persson (2003 forthcoming), 'The gains from pension reform?', *Journal of Economic Literature*.

Lindbeck, A. and D. Snower (2000), 'Multitask learning and the reorganization of work: from Tayloristic to holistic organizations', *Journal of Labor Economics*, 19: 353–376.

Lindbeck, A. and S. Wikström (2000), 'The ICT revolution in consumer product markets', *Consumption, Markets and Culture*, 4: 77–99.

(2002), 'E-exchange and the boundary between households and organizations', CESifo Working Paper No. 806, Munich: CESifo.

Martin, J. M. and D. Grubb (2001), 'What works and for whom: a review of OECD countries' experiences with active labour market policies' (mimeo), Office of Labour Market Policy Evaluation (IFAU), Uppsala.

McHale, J. (1999), 'The risk of social security benefit rule changes: some international evidence', NBER Working Paper No. 7031, National Bureau of Economic Research, Cambridge, MA.

Nicoletti, G., R. D. G. Haffner, S. Nickell, S. Scarpetta and G. Zoega (2001), 'European integration, liberalization, and labor-market performance', in G. Bertola, T. Boeri and G. Nicoletti, *Welfare and unemployment in a united Europe*, Cambridge, MA: MIT Press, pp. 147–236.

OECD (2002), *Social Expenditures*, database.

RFV [Riksförsäkringsverket] (2002a), 'Sjukskrivnas syn på hälsa och arbete' [Attitudes towards health and work of individuals on sick leave], *Analysera* 2002:16, Working Paper, Stockholm: RFV.

(2002b), 'Svensk sjukfrånvaro i ett europeiskt perspektiv' [sick absenteeism in Sweden in a European perspective], *Analysera* 2002:11, Working Paper, Stockholm: RFV.

Rosen, S. (1997), 'Public employment and the welfare state in Sweden', in R. Freeman, B. Swedenborg and R. Topel (eds.), *Reforming the welfare state: the Swedish model in transition*, Chicago: NBER and University of Chicago Press, pp. 79–108.

Sinn, H. W. (2000), 'The threat to the German welfare state', CESifo Working Paper No. 320, Munich: CESifo.

Skogman Thoursie, P. (2002), 'Reporting sick: are sporting events contagious?' (mimeo), Department of Economics, Stockholm University.

3 | Integrating and liberalizing the market for network services: gas and electricity

Introduction

The Single European Act mandated the European Commission to propose policies to bring about a single market in financial services, gas, electricity, transport and telecommunications. The Commission has been remarkably successful in issuing directives with that intent, and is now focused more on ensuring that the directives are implemented, and where necessary strengthened to achieve their purpose.

Different countries have embraced this reform programme with differing degrees of enthusiasm, with Britain, the Nordic countries and Spain in the vanguard but others more cautious. In the past, state-owned utilities were restricted to operating within their national frontiers. Part of the pressure for extending and accelerating market liberalization comes from newly privatized companies that are seeking to diversify out of their national markets. Some continental countries, notably France, have not restricted their still state-owned utilities from foreign ventures, and have undoubtedly benefited from a largely protected home market and access to cheaper, de facto state-guaranteed finance. The imbalance this creates for competition is a source of considerable tension within the EU, and a strong reason for further liberalization and harmonization, so that companies in the same industry face similar competitive conditions across the Union.

Paper presented at the IESE conference on Building a More Dynamic Europe, Barcelona, 27 November 2001. Support from the ESRC under the project R000 238563 *Efficient and sustainable regulation and competition in network industries*, is gratefully acknowledged. Jordi Gual, Karsten Neuhoff and Tanga McDaniel provided helpful comments. An earlier version was published as Newbery, 2002, and is reprinted here with the permission of Elsevier.

The underlying case for liberalizing network industries is that it allows competitive pressure to be put on sleepy monopolies, and restricts cross-subsidies that frequently take the form of a tax on competitive medium-sized industry to subsidize domestic consumers (and sometimes politically powerful large business). In some sectors – notably telecoms, where technical progress is rapid – competition is the best way of identifying winners and enabling them to replace losers. In other sectors with high capital investment needs (such as water or rail), private finance is seen in many countries as the most likely to deliver the investment in a timely and cost-effective manner without entangling the public sector in difficult macroeconomic financing decisions. In road transport, however, public infrastructural investment is still required, and its delivery is proving difficult, while the variety of methods chosen by governments to tax and finance roads creates further tensions for the single transport market.

Policy towards many network utilities involves more than purely economic and efficiency considerations. Energy is a matter of national security, service obligations, affordability and environmental impact. Telecoms is increasingly part of a converged communications industry, where control over distribution of content raises issues of political accountability, privacy and security. The proper regulation of financial services against fraud, to encourage proper corporate governance while promoting efficient investment and protecting minority shareholders, is critical to efficient investment and hence national performance. As financial services are a footloose service industry, there are potentially great gains to individual countries in strengthening their financial centres, but this may be largely at the expense of other countries. Countries that fear they may lose may resist reforms, impeding the gains from better regulation and restructuring.

Perhaps as a result, the current challenge is to find ways of increasing the effectiveness of competition in delivering efficiency without compromising other goals that are thought to be nationally important. Regulating networks to improve the *efficiency* of competitive outcomes is not necessarily the same as maximizing the degree of liberalization. Nor is merger policy that was designed for normal industries necessarily well suited to addressing mergers in network industries, and here the tension between member states and the Commission is likely to become acute in some cases.

Reforming network utilities

In a short chapter it is impossible to do justice to all the steps that are needed to improve the workings of the single market in services. Instead, I concentrate on four key issues: *regulation, restructuring* and the related issues of *risk management* and ensuring effective sustainable *competition* in the context of the special characteristics of network utilities, although some of the lessons may also apply to aspects of financial markets (where cash points and settlement systems have some similarities with utility networks). These principles are then illustrated for the two key energy sectors of gas and electricity, which are the subject of a proposed new directive.

One of the main distinguishing characteristics of network utilities is that the network is potentially an 'essential facility'. A facility is essential if competitors require access to the facility if they are to be able to offer their service to final consumers, and if it would be impossible or prohibitively expensive to duplicate the facility. Networks (or in some cases parts of the network, such as the 'last mile' or local loop in telecommunications or call termination in mobile telephony) usually fall into this category, as the network is normally a natural monopoly whose duplication would be excessively expensive and hence inefficient. In most developed jurisdictions, competition laws require that those who own or control essential facilities may be obliged to grant access to competitors where denial of access would have serious effects on competition. This obligation to grant access arises only where downstream competition is possible and only in cases where access to the facility is essential to enable that competition to take place.

Essential facilities occur outside the conventional public network utilities, and are then subject to competition law, in the EU under Article 82, which prohibits the abuse of a dominant position. If a party owns, or controls access to, an essential facility and denies that access to service providers who can deliver services to downstream consumers only if granted access to that facility, then that party would be in breach of Article 82 and would be abusing its dominant position (unless refusal could be objectively justified, for example, because of inadequate capacity).

In the past network utilities were typically granted monopoly franchises and hence downstream competition was not possible, and the essential facilities doctrine did not apply. In exchange for the grant of a monopoly franchise, the utility was either regulated or, more usually, under state ownership with a mandate to operate in the public interest and not just to extract the monopoly rents that control over the essential facility potentially allows. These franchise monopolies were typically vertically integrated (so that the natural monopoly was bundled with service provision). They were regional or national in scope, and traded with each other where necessary under bilateral agreements. The growing evidence of the beneficial effects of liberalization, first in telecoms and subsequently in electricity and gas, suggested to the Commission that 'market forces produce a better allocation of resources and greater effectiveness in the supply of services',[1] and that therefore the principles of the single market – 'the free movement of goods, persons, services and capital'[2] – should be extended to these public utilities. Competition in supply makes key network elements into essential facilities, to which the principles of Article 82 should logically apply.

In practice, the European Commission has articulated more specific requirements for individual network utilities in directives to make clear what would or would not be an abuse of dominant position. Thus the Commission has spelt out how this would apply to the telecommunications sector (in OJ No. C233/2, 6 September 1991): it would be unlawful for a telecommunications company to refuse to provide reserved services (those in which it still has a monopoly) when it would make it impossible or difficult for competitors to provide non-reserved services.

Regulation

Network industries require suitably staffed, independent but accountable national regulatory authorities (NRAs) with adequate powers of ex ante regulation. Competition law under Articles 81 and 82 may provide a useful framework, but actions to address market abuse under these articles is bureaucratic, slow and limited in the range of remedies available. Ex ante regulatory powers are particularly important in the early learning period of utility restructuring, when the details of market

---

[1] EC communication, *Services of general interest in Europe*, OJ No. C281, 26 September 1996, p. 3.
[2] Article 7A of the EC Treaty.

design and the rights and obligations of market participants need to be adjusted in the light of experience both within the country and from elsewhere.

The three main regulatory problems are that in some countries there is no NRA (e.g., there is no NRA for gas or electricity in Germany); in other countries the NRA is not sufficiently independent of the state, which is particularly problematic where the state retains a majority ownership in the utility being regulated (e.g., France); and finally, in some countries the legislative powers of the regulator are inadequate to the purpose. Even where the regulator has adequate powers to control the natural monopoly components, he may lack essential powers (of the kind normally set out in licence conditions) to deal with the potentially competitive service markets, and this is addressed under that heading below (pp. 90–94).

There are a number of less structural but still significant regulatory issues to resolve. To be effective, regulation should be credible and predictable. Regulatory credibility suffered a serious setback in Britain when the government forced Railtrack into administration – a move perceived by many to involve overruling the regulator's duty to ensure that the regulated utility, Railtrack, was able to finance its licensed operations. It remains unclear whether the motive for liquidation was to replace failing management, or a decision that the structure was inappropriate and should be replaced by non-legislative means. Whether the reduction in regulatory credibility extends beyond railways is unclear – other utilities require no government subsidy and the regulatory task is to restrain prices from excessive levels. The problem in the railway industry is that even profit-maximizing prices fail to cover costs, given the strong competition from road transport (despite the high taxes on that sector). The government is therefore continuously in the position of paymaster. Independent regulation may not be a plausible option in such circumstances. If so, it is important to learn the lessons and devise suitable ownership and governance structures for railways if that aspect of the single transport market is to be encouraged.

One of the main sources of regulatory uncertainty is the status of future environmental policy and requirements, particularly in the energy industries where important investment decisions must be made on expectations of future fuel prices. Governments have largely failed to agree on an appropriate climate change policy. They appear undecided as to whether this should be implemented by the most logical

solution of carbon taxes on all fuels, or through more discriminatory and relatively illogical and hence unstable interventions such as
the climate change levy in Britain, emissions trading, green tickets or
favourable subsidies to renewables (but not to large hydro). It does
not help that trading regimes for electricity may penalize unpredictable
energy sources such as wind – a victim of the New Electricity Trading
Arrangements in Britain. Combined heat and power (CHP) systems enjoy a variety of relatively unstable tax advantages in various countries,
making the necessarily durable investment decisions in this technology
particularly fraught.

Regulators are poorly placed to give clear signals when the tax and
legislative uncertainties are as great as they are, and rapid progress
towards an intelligent and efficient environmental policy would do
much to reduce risks in energy investment. Unfortunately, given the
great variety of existing energy resources (nuclear in France, gas in the
Netherlands, hydro in Scandinavia, coal in Germany and Britain), only
an optimist would anticipate such a policy emerging smoothly. With
the common agricultural policy as an awful lesson, the challenge to
the European Union is to demonstrate that it can achieve a rational
set of policies towards the environment and hence reduce some of the
uncertainty that prevents efficient investment decision-making across
the single market.

Restructuring and ownership separation

The process of ensuring effective and efficient competition in network
utilities in the presence of essential facilities is not straightforward. The
logical solution to ensure open, transparent and non-discriminatory access to the essential facility or network is to unbundle the industry and
insist on ownership separation – that is, the party that owns or controls
the essential facility should have no ownership stake in or ability to
control the potentially competitive services. In electricity, this would
prevent transmission or distribution network operators from having
ownership stakes in generation and supply (that is, retailing to final
consumers), while telecoms companies would have to choose between
operating the local loop and providing telephone services over the local
loop. The main issue in restructuring utilities is to balance the synergies
of vertical integration against the benefits of more equal competition,
freed from the bias of incumbent ownership of the essential facility.

Synergies of vertical integration

The apparently logical solution of ownership unbundling runs into problems if there are significant synergies or economies of scope in operating the network and providing services over it. Thus in the public switched telephone network, the operator must set up a circuit from the caller to the called party by routeing the call through switches and maintaining the integrity of that circuit for the duration of the call. Owning and using these switches provides natural synergies. Similarly, the system operator of an electricity system must ensure that supply and demand are kept continuously in balance millisecond by millisecond, and therefore needs very tight control over generation. The gas transmission operator must maintain the correct pressure in all pipelines from well head to burner tip, as a loss of pressure could cause an ingress of air and lead to explosions. In the past, the required close coordination between production (of electricity or gas) and operation of the transmission network has been facilitated by vertically integrating the activities under common ownership. If they are separated, that coordination will have to be achieved by contracts and market signals, with an inevitable increase in transaction and other costs.[3] In some cases, the extra transaction costs would be so high that it would be more efficient to retain common ownership. In other cases, the transaction costs are more modest, while the improvements in efficiency from allowing competition and market discovery to reallocate resources and drive down costs considerably outweigh the extra transaction costs.

If the owner of the essential facility also provides services over the essential facility that are in competition with those offered by potential entrants, then it will have powerful incentives to discourage entry or discriminate against successful entrants. Abuse of the dominant

---

[3] The contract costs incurred by 2002 for unbundling track assets and contracting for services on the London Underground had already reached 600 million euros, while the costs of changing the electricity trading arrangements in Britain in 2001 have been estimated at 1.5 billion euros. Clearly contracting costs can be very substantial. The other costs include those of inefficient decisions guided by imperfect prices or contractual details between the formerly integrated parts of the business. On the other hand, greater clarity in the nature of some costs can improve the efficiency of network management. Compensating train operators for delays caused by the rail track company may lead to more efficient scheduling of maintenance.

position provided by an essential facility is illegal, but it may be extremely difficult for competition authorities or regulators to distinguish between access charges that are cost-justified (or can be objectively justified) and those that are (unreasonably) discriminatory. Equally it may be hard to distinguish between access terms that can be technically justified and those that have been devised purely for commercial advantage. Many of the complaints about delays in liberalization and impediments to open, transparent and non-discriminatory access fall into this category (see, for a good set of examples, the Sixth Report on the Implementation of the Telecommunications Regulatory Package, COM (2000) 818 of 7 December 2000).[4]

Whether and under what circumstances ownership unbundling is cost-effective is an empirical question, the answer to which may change as a result of technical progress. Commission directives attempt to summarize the present state of knowledge in the belief that the experience from some cases or countries can be applied elsewhere in the EU (even if not necessarily to countries at lower levels of development). Many of the tensions experienced during the liberalization process arise because of disagreements about the applicability of lessons from earlier reforms, or even what lessons can be drawn from particular experiences.

The electricity supply industry provides a good example. In a mature and densely meshed network, with adequate transmission capacity and few transmission constraints, and adequate generation capacity with a generous reserve margin, there is a strong case for ownership unbundling of transmission and generation, following the model adopted by the restructuring of the Central Electricity Generating Board of England and Wales in 1990. Provided there is adequate competition, discussed below (pp. 90–94), generators can then bid to deliver electricity to final consumers using the grid under regulated third-party access (where access and transmission charges are regulated and published in advance). The system operator secures the various ancillary services needed to maintain the quality of supply (frequency, voltage, instantaneous balance, spinning reserves and reserves available over varying time periods). The previous system in which investment in transmission and generation was simultaneously determined by

---

[4] See http://europa.eu.int/ISPO/infosoc/telecompolicy/implrep6/com2000-814en.pdf.

the integrated monopoly can in theory be replaced by decentralized mechanisms. Well-designed charges for access and transmission combined with a competitive wholesale market could then guide new investment in a timely manner to the least-cost location.

In smaller systems where individual investments are large relative to total capacity, and/or where the least-cost plant has high fixed costs and long lead times (quintessentially, nuclear power stations or large coal-fired power stations), the benefits of tight co-ordination between investment decisions in transmission and generation can be significant. Centralized planning may allow the system to be operated with lower reserves and hence lower cost, but with less flexibility than would be desirable in a liberalized market (as I shall discuss below, pp. 82–83). The efficiency gains of competition need to exceed the extra costs (of the new markets themselves, as well as the additional spare capacity to ensure liquid and competitive markets) for unbundling to be cost-effective. Thus the argument that ownership unbundling is necessarily desirable for electricity is not absolute, but contingent upon prevailing circumstances. In the EU, the benefits of improving interconnection between countries and the present levels of transmission adequacy and generation reserve strongly suggest that the competitive benefits of ownership unbundling greatly outweigh the loss of synergies in tight ownership control over transmission and generation. That view is resisted in France, where Electricité de France (EdF) argues that its preponderance of inflexible nuclear power stations requires far tighter co-ordination between transmission and generation than in other EU electricity markets. These issues are discussed below (pp. 89–97) in the context of proposed reforms to the Electricity Directive, and suggest that striking the right balance between the benefits of introducing competition against the increased costs of vertical separation cannot be taken as axiomatic but will depend on the evidence.

Circuit-switched telephony (both fixed-line and mobile) exhibits strong synergies between network operation and service provision. The information needed to bill customers is collected at the same time as the circuit is set up between switches, and has in the past argued for the local area network provider to also offer local telephony services. In the United States, the Modified Final Judgement separated AT&T's long-distance lines from the local Bell Operating Companies in 1984, thus allowing competition for long-distance traffic. Other operators could offer phone services, but had to make access payments for origination and termination to the local Bell company, allowing the partial unbundling of service and network.

Technical progress that made long-distance telephony contestable has continued, and the growing range of methods of handling calls to final customers (by cable, wireless and possibly even power lines) is increasingly making the local telephone service contestable, allowing the possibility of facilities-based competition between different service providers. Once this is economic, the network ceases to be an essential facility and, if competition from alternative providers is sufficiently intense, may reduce the need for network regulation.

New bottlenecks may, however, replace the old essential facility of the local loop. Once a customer has chosen between alternative facilities for delivering calls, then that facility provider controls the bottleneck of call termination and origination with that customer. Whether this creates the potential for abusing a dominant position or not depends very much on the contestability of that facility, which may in turn depend upon who pays for its use. Mobile network operators (MNOs) are arguing with the Commission and many national regulatory agencies about whether call termination to mobile phones is an essential facility that needs to be regulated, or whether the high churn rate and intense competition between MNOs ensures that the total price for using mobiles is kept at competitive levels, possibly with a different balance between origination and termination charges than might be imposed by a perfectly informed welfare-maximizing regulator.

Vertical integration is likely to lead to an attempt to load as many costs on to the bottleneck element as possible, allowing the incumbent's competitive service to be cross-subsidized, thus deterring entry and restricting competition. Where facilities-based competition is possible, inefficient cross-subsidies will be constrained, and the benefits of the resulting competition may outweigh the apparent extra costs of duplicating facilities, to which must be added the possible considerable costs of regulating access charges and conditions. These costs can be high, particularly as they can delay or deter innovation, and may argue against enforced sharing of network elements. Where facilities-based competition is not sensible, ownership unbundling may be justified, and here the extra transaction costs need to be balanced against the extra costs of regulating access and dealing with the strong incentives to discriminate. Again, these costs can be high, and need to be added to the other benefits from non-discriminatory competition when deciding on the desirability of ownership unbundling.

Efficient restructuring choices

The two problems to address in choosing the desirable degree of ownership unbundling are, first, to decide the most suitable structure of vertical relations between the essential facility or natural monopoly elements of the industry and the potentially competitive services that require access to the essential facility and, second, to determine how best to achieve this, given the current ownership structure. For the energy industries of electricity and gas, there is considerable evidence and widespread agreement that upstream production should be under separate ownership from transmission and distribution. There remains some ambiguity about the appropriate relationship between the transmission owner and the system operator, who may need extensive control over some production units to provide balancing and ancillary services. Whether these should be secured from separate owners under contract and through spot markets or by direct control of some owned assets (such as pumped storage units) may depend on the system architecture and fuels available. There is less agreement about the desirable degree of separation between distribution and downstream supply (retailing to final customers); this is discussed in detail for the case of the electricity industry below (pp. 82–83), but applies equally for gas.

In the case of telecommunications, the structural questions are rather different, and relate to the best route to liberalization. Complete vertical separation appears unattractive, and the question is whether to aim at facilities-based competition or to enforce various forms of unbundling, particularly of the local loop. Mobile telephony started with facilities-based competition, though with access to existing facilities for some entrants. The issue here is the extent to which facilities may be shared to reduce the cost of 3-G roll-out (the deployment of multimedia mobile telephony).

There is even less agreement and insufficient evidence to determine the best structure for railways. The directive requires functional unbundling between track infrastructure and services offered over the track (by train operating companies, or TOCs). Clearly, a single market requires a degree of interoperability so that TOCs can access tracks in other countries. It is less clear whether the British solution of complete vertical separation between track and TOCs is efficient or sustainable. The collapse of Railtrack and the difficulty of financing the West Coast upgrade to allow the TOC Virgin to operate high-speed tilting trains led to contractual risk sharing for that investment, suggesting that synergies between track and TOC are important, particularly for new investment. The future structure of British railways is unclear, but may evolve towards regional vertically integrated track and train companies. Arguably the more important integration to secure is between track and track maintenance companies, which was severed with unfortunate consequences in Britain.

Finally, the water industry remains vertically integrated for the most part on the water supply side, though in Britain some companies combine sewerage operations, while others delegate these to the regional water and sewerage company. Attempts to introduce competition upstream have had limited success, constrained by the economics where the main cost lies in transport and distribution and not in production (except for new supplies in some areas). The high cost of metering and ensuring quality standards further limits the prospects for competition where facilities must be shared.

The problem of transition to the new structure
The best time to make structural changes is at (or before) privatization, but that lesson has been largely ignored. Britain sold telecoms and gas as vertically integrated monopolies, and only unbundled electricity and rail after many years of regulatory experience. The directives forced a rapid pace of reform on member states, giving them little time to resolve the debate between those arguing for national champions, those resisting any structural change and those concerned to deliver competitive microeconomic foundations for their service sector. In some countries the problem of transition was complicated by municipal or regional-level ownership and prior private ownership. Few countries have enthusiastically embraced the need to compensate for stranded assets, which might be involved in extensive divestiture, particularly as the gainers from liberalization are more likely to be the commercial and industrial sector than the voting public. The alternative is to impose sufficient regulatory pressure and require legal separation in the hope that this will encourage the companies to voluntarily accept full ownership separation as a way of escaping increasingly onerous regulation. That is likely to take time, judging from UK and US experience.

The issue is further discussed in the section on gas restructuring below (pp. 85–88).

Unbundling, risk and contracts

Unbundling vertically integrated companies creates transactions between the upstream and downstream parties that were previously internalized and offsetting. In some cases, notably the electricity market, the market-clearing spot price for these transactions will be extremely volatile and creates significant risk. When capacity is tight, electricity spot prices can easily exceed 1,000 euros/MWh, but with adequate capacity off-peak prices may fall to the variable cost of the least-cost generation plant (15–20 euros/MWh), well below the price needed to cover the fixed costs. Customers face the risk of volatile and occasionally extremely high prices, while generators face the risk of sustained periods of low average prices failing to recover their investment costs.

The natural instrument to hedge these risks is a contract between the generator and the final customer (often with intermediate contracts involving suppliers). Where the utility is vertically integrated and regulated, regulation (or state ownership) normally guarantees stable and predictable final consumer prices, possibly periodically adjusted to changes in fuel costs (which for domestic customers may amount to only one-quarter of the total price). In effect consumers are covered by implicit long-term or undated contracts, which are well suited to financing the very durable infrastructural investment in transmission and generation. In the case of gas, investments in pipelines were, and to a considerable extent still are, financed on the back of twenty-year contracts for transport, and similarly gas wells were developed on the back of long-term contracts, often linked to the transport contracts.

Unbundling typically greatly shortens the duration of contracts, often to as little as six months to two years. This period is sufficient to deal with daily volatility of the kind found in electricity spot markets, but does not deal with the longer-term volatility associated with variations in the capacity–demand margin. Private investors will be wary of speculatively financing infrastructure, particularly in transmission, without some assurance that it will be allowed to earn an acceptable return. Where wholesale and retail markets are competitive and liquid, investors can assess the commercial risks involved in investing to increase supply ahead of projected increases in demand. Where transmission is regulated under credible cost-reflective tariffs the same may also be true. However, regulators are under a variety of pressures to meet environmental objectives, protect vulnerable consumers and ensure security of supply in the face of international energy disruptions, as well as having a duty to deliver prices as low as possible to final consumers. Investors in some countries which have yet to develop a tradition of independent and economically rational regulation may be reluctant to forgo the security of commercially enforceable long-term contracts, particularly for gas.

The problem is that long-term contracts can pre-empt capacity in transmission and effectively foreclose the market, reducing competition. There is therefore a tension between a desire for liberalized markets supporting a variety of contracts of varying lengths, and the present situation which, particularly in the gas market, is relatively inflexible and resistant to competitive pressure. Again, achieving the right balance between the benefits of risk reduction that long-term contracts provide and the opportunities for market foreclosure that pre-emptive capacity contracting may offer lies at the heart of many disputes over opening up markets.

Sustaining effective competition over networks

The Californian electricity crisis, described below (pp. 96–97), reminds us that short-run demand elasticities are very low, transmission constraints fragment markets, and within these fragmented markets individual producers may have considerable if temporary market power, and spot prices in these markets can reach very high levels. Sustained periods of shortages caused by underinvestment or adverse hydrological conditions may mean that market-clearing prices can remain at high levels for lengthy periods and can produce politically unsustainable final prices to voting consumers.

This problem is peculiar to energy markets, as other network utilities do not have the same spot wholesale markets whose prices feed directly through to final consumer prices. Ensuring adequate competition to prevent the exploitation of transient market power is difficult enough, but in many national markets the number of major energy producers is sufficiently small that normal problems of market power can be expected, particularly as demand grows and capacity is retired, replacing the present glut of capacity with tighter markets in future.

Past directives appear to take the view that normal competition law is adequate for the unregulated or potentially competitive parts of the market, such as wholesale electricity production and gas production. The directives are therefore concentrated on structural reforms and access regulation. If liberalization is to deliver the promised efficiency gains, though, considerably more attention must be paid to ensuring that the potentially competitive markets are effectively competitive, and this will have consequential implications for how they and the networks are regulated.

Reforming the Electricity and Gas Directives

The four issues of reforming regulation, restructuring, managing risk and ensuring effective competition are conveniently illustrated by the case of the gas and electricity industries, both the subject of proposed reforms of the energy directives. The original Electricity Directive 96/92/EC was much influenced by the success of restructuring the electricity supply industry in Britain, which demonstrated the superiority of unbundling (the model followed in England and Wales) compared to the Scottish model of privatizing vertically integrated regional companies (Newbery, 2000). The Electricity Directive 96/92/EC and Gas Directive 98/30/EC were adopted in 1996 and 1998, and had to be implemented by February 1999 and August 2000 respectively.

In late 1998, a group of academics undertook a study of the rationale of, progress of and possible problems with implementing the Electricity Directive. The resulting book, *A European market for electricity?* (Bergman *et al.*, 1999), drew attention to a number of unsatisfactory aspects of the reforms. Very similar conclusions were subsequently drawn by the European Council, which called on the Commission to accelerate the work to complete the internal market in electricity and gas at Lisbon in March 2000. Gas liberalization had been considerably more contentious because of perceived issues of security of supply, and it had taken eight years to introduce a relatively less demanding directive compared to electricity, but the European Parliament was anxious to completely liberalize both energy markets.[5]

[5] Resolution 'Liberalisation of Energy Markets', A5-0180/2000, 6 July 2000.

In response the Commission proposed amending the two directives at the European Council in Stockholm in March 2001.[6] The main changes proposed were to require *regulated* third-party access (TPA) for both gas and electricity (denying the former option of negotiated TPA), to strengthen the requirements for unbundling to legal (but not necessarily ownership) separation of generation and transmission, to remove the option of the single-buyer model and to allow all gas and electricity customers freedom to choose their supplier by 1 January 2005, thus ending the domestic customer franchise monopoly. In addition the directive would require all countries to establish independent regulators to approve transport tariffs ex ante, and to monitor and report to the Commission on the state of electricity and gas markets, particularly the supply/demand balance.

France, which missed the deadline for enacting the earlier directives, and has done minimal restructuring and market opening, opposed the proposals, arguing that it was too soon to deem energy liberalization a success. Germany, with its preference for negotiated TPA and vertical integration, also opposed the proposals, particularly the requirement for an independent regulator. The proposals were discussed at the Barcelona Council Meeting of 15–16 March 2002, which resolved to open markets to non-domestic customers by 2004. Finally, after further proposals were published in June 2002, the energy ministers agreed on 25 November 2002 to full domestic liberalization from 1 July 2007 (in Article 21 of the amended directive).

Opening the gas market

The gas market is central to Europe's energy needs and security concerns. Effective liberalization could transform the industry, dramatically lower prices and reduce EU import bills. At present the price of gas is linked to the price of oil, rather than being determined by supply and demand in a competitive market. The link to the oil price is a relic of the period when the price of gas was based on its value to the consumer rather than on the cost of production (including scarcity rents) and dates from the period when pipelines and wells were

---

[6] COM(2001) 125 final, 13 March 2001; available together with the Press Release and Working Paper at http://europa.eu.int/comm/energy/en/internal-market/int-market.html.

financed on long-term take-or-pay contracts with an objectively enforceable price clause. Internationally traded oil was the logical index
that satisfied the value-based pricing rule and could be contractually
enforced.[7]

The potentially dramatic effects of unbundling and competition can
be seen from Britain before the interconnector to the continent was
opened up in 2001. During the period from 1994 to 2000, the price of
gas fell dramatically and it was only the opening of the interconnector and the ability to export to the oil-based pricing regime in Europe
that caused prices to double. Gas-on-gas competition is facilitated by
a densely meshed high-pressure pipeline system and a sufficient number of competing producers. When they sell into a market in which
combined-cycle gas turbines are the least-cost option for investment
and have to compete against coal generation for dispatch the stage
is set for sustainably low gas prices. If the major suppliers to the EU
(Russia, Algeria, Norway and Libya) have to compete with each other
and against coal in the electricity market, with liquid spot forward and
futures markets, then they may be forced to accept a loss of linkage
to the oil price. As international trade in liquefied natural gas moves
from long-term contracts to a more liquid spot market, that tendency
will be reinforced.

The reality is still a long way from this vision. The EU commissioned a report into the opening of the gas market (DRI.WEFA, 2001)
which shows the considerable obstacles that remain in liberalizing the
gas market. The main barrier to competition is restricted access to the
grid, difficulties in obtaining gas and vertical integration. The report
notes that there has been to date no significant downward pressure
on transportation and distribution costs and no fundamental move
from oil-linked pricing towards long-run marginal cost-based pricing. Perhaps this is not surprising, as the only country with ownership unbundling is the UK, and only seven countries (Finland, Ireland,

---

[7] Value-based pricing in its purest form means estimating the highest price
the gas buyer will pay rather than switch to the next best fuel, which for
many (but not all) purposes is oil. Oil-linked gas prices produce major distortions in the electricity generation sector where the practical alternative is
normally coal, a fuel whose price is relatively independent of the oil price.
Oil has the additional attraction as an index in visibility, and preserving
the concept of gas as a premium fuel.

Italy, Luxembourg, Spain, Sweden, and the UK) have regulated third-party access. Germany lacks a regulator, while the score card of operators' experience of accessing the grid as of March 2001 is poor in all countries except the UK, and particularly poor in Belgium and Germany, with the Netherlands scoring the lowest mark on the balancing regime.[8]

Gas exhibits all of the problems that control over the essential facilities of transmission, balancing and storage provides to an incumbent determined to protect the market against competition. Britain demonstrated the difficulties of ownership restructuring in a privatized market, and unfortunately many gas companies on the continent are partly or wholly privately owned. Britain privatized British Gas as a vertically integrated monopoly in 1984, and spent the next fifteen years applying regulatory pressure and references to the Monopolies and Mergers Commission to enforce a regime in which ownership unbundling was considered the least unattractive option by the owner. That was in the context in which Britain was self-sufficient in gas and not reliant upon imports from politically unstable regions to the east. The argument that long-term contracting supported by massively capitalized, vertically integrated national champions is the only way to ensure security of supply is difficult to refute in the absence of convincing models demonstrating the alternative.

As with electricity, discussed below (pp. 89–97), there are sound reasons for continuing with some long-term contracts, and this strongly suggests retaining the domestic franchise for gas. The ideal is to separate transmission and distribution from production and supply (including the management of long-term contracts with the distribution companies) to remove the incentives for exploiting and abusing essential facilities.

---

[8] The balancing regime is the set of terms and conditions under which balancing services are offered to customers. These services are required if the amount contracted differs from the amount actually taken over some time period, either because of individual supply or demand problems or a failure to predict demand accurately. Such services are normally offered by the pipeline operator drawing upon short-term reserves, or securing offsetting balances from other agents. The supply of such services may be bundled with the natural monopoly network service, though they may be secured in a balancing market.

One effective way in which dominant incumbents can exert market power is through unreasonable pricing for ancillary services such as balancing and storage, and excessive charges for transmission and distribution. These charges can have very adverse effects on the efficient operation of the electricity market, where access to short-term gas for supplying electricity into a short-term spot or balancing market may be critical to prevent electricity price spikes. Under some systems of gas-balancing charges, notably those in the Netherlands, the price for such gas can be so high as to either pass spikes through to the electricity market or cause suppliers to withhold their generation, amplifying the problems in the electricity spot market. It will take knowledgeable and well-informed regulators armed with considerable regulatory powers to align the prices for various gas services towards costs and improve the liquidity of gas spot and contract markets.

During 2002 the Commission prepared a sequence of amendments to the Gas Directive, with the intention of adapting the rules for electricity and gas. On 27 November 2002, the energy ministers agreed to a new 'consolidated proposal' for a directive with annexes covering gas and electricity. This will open markets to all non-domestic customers by 1 July 2004 and to all customers by 1 July 2007. The new proposal strengthens the requirement of non-discriminatory access to transmission and storage, and specifically requires that the transmission operator should be 'independent at least in terms of its legal form, organisation and decision making from other activities not connected with transmission' (Article 9). This does not, however, require ownership unbundling. In addition 'Member States shall ensure the implementation of a system of third party access to the transmission and distribution system, and LNG facilities, based on published tariffs, applicable to all eligible customers' (Article 18), though access to storage can still be on a negotiated basis (Article 19). The methodology for these tariffs will be set by 'competent bodies with the function of regulatory authorities . . . wholly independent of the interests of the gas industry' (Article 25). The spirit of this new directive, and particularly the move to regulated third-party access and national regulatory authorities, should have a dramatic effect on the European gas sector. It still needs to be incorporated into member states' legislation, and its success may be limited if there are significant derogations for long-term contracts and capacity adequacy.

Reforming electricity markets

All the Commission documents on its website go to some lengths to argue that the proposed measures for the European energy market 'will avoid the type of problems currently faced by California, which have resulted from an inadequate legal framework and inadequate production capacity' (EC Press Release). Clearly, the Californian electricity crisis has awakened fears that liberalized electricity markets may be politically unsustainable, at least without careful design and regulation. The very high prices observed in California (and in the north- and mid-west of the United States) have demonstrated very clearly that the scarcity price of electricity can reach extremely high levels when supply is tight. Defenders of the former electricity industry structure have argued that vertically integrated franchise monopolies with regulated final prices are the only politically sustainable structure, which is necessary to secure adequate capacity to avoid shortages and/or high prices (see, e.g., the pseudonymous Price C. Watts, 2001). The cost of flawed liberalization has now been demonstrated (by the high prices and the impact on economic activity in the event of power outages) to be unacceptably high, and calls into question the whole electricity liberalization agenda.

The evidence from Europe and the United States suggests that there are a number of conditions for successfully liberalizing gas and electricity markets. The first is that, for the wholesale market to be competitive, potential suppliers must have access to the transmission system in order to reach customers. This is best achieved by ownership separation of transmission (and distribution) from generation. Newbery (2000), drawing on earlier work (Newbery and Pollitt, 1997) and work by Pollitt (Domah and Pollitt, 2001), contrasts the success of this strategy in England and Wales (a permanent annual reduction of costs of 6 per cent compared to the no-reform counterfactual) with the failure of privatization in Scotland, which left the two incumbent vertically integrated utilities unchanged. In a federal (or multi-country) market such as the EU, this requires that suppliers, traders and consumers can gain access to trading partners in and through other countries. This lesson has been endorsed by the Commission.

The second condition is that there is adequate and secure supply. For electricity, there are three conditions that need to be satisfied for supply security: the network infrastructure must be adequate and reliable;[9] there is adequate generation capacity;[10] and there is security of supply of the primary fuels (gas, oil, coal etc.). In the case of gas, supply security means that pipeline integrity and pressure must be maintained (normally through a combination of line-pack, swing, short-, medium- and longer-duration storage,[11] and interruptible contracts); that adequate supplies are available, often underwritten by long-term contracts; and that the risks of interruption to these sources of supply have been addressed (particularly those involving imports from, or transit through, politically unstable regimes). Again, this is recognized by the Commission.

The final condition is that there is appropriate regulation of the markets of these liberalized utilities. This condition is less obvious, and has not been adequately addressed by some EU countries but, without it, there are serious risks that the benefits of liberalization may be lost, and the political costs of flawed outcomes may undermine support for reform.

Regulating wholesale markets

The mantra 'competition where feasible, regulation where not' suggests that regulation should be confined to the natural monopoly elements, typically the networks. That would be mistaken, for the potentially competitive elements still need regulatory oversight to ensure that markets are not manipulated or market power abused. The default assumption is that wholesale gas and electricity markets are no different from other markets, and should therefore be subject to the same competition law as other markets, notably Articles 81 and 82 of the Treaty, which have been transcribed into national legislation (e.g., as

[9] In practice, this means that the grid is built to an n–1 standard, allowing any circuit to fail without causing system breakdown.
[10] The reserve margin required will depend upon the reliability of the generation units, the variability of demand, and the response speed of the generation units, and should be available for at least the specified (and very high) fraction of the time so that the risk of capacity shortfall is less than a specified level.
[11] Line-pack, or variations in pipeline pressure, deals with daily variations in demand, swing is the ability of production to vary with demand, and storage is characterized by volume and deliverability, usually in inverse relationship.

the Competition Act 1998 in the UK). There are a number of obvious problems with this approach. First, because it is ex post and penalty-based, it is necessarily legalistic and inevitably slow compared to ex ante regulation. Second, the EU test of abuse of dominant position normally requires the dominant firm to have 40 per cent or more of the relevant market. Defining a market that is so dominated can be problematic. Third, the presumption is that normally markets will be effectively competitive, so that the information needed to establish market abuse is not collected routinely, but only when an alleged abuse is investigated.

The British energy regulator, Ofgem, with over a decade of experience of dealing with the initially concentrated wholesale gas and electricity markets, is acutely aware of the limitations of normal competition legislation. In 2000, Ofgem persuaded the majority of large electricity generating companies to accept the market abuse licence condition (MALC), which specified certain forms of behaviour as *prima facie* abusive, meriting investigation and possible penalty. Two generators, AES (with 7 per cent of total capacity, mostly under long-term sales contracts) and British Energy (with overwhelmingly base-load inflexible nuclear power) did not consider the change in licence conditions necessary and appealed to the Competition Commission. The condition related to behaviour in the Electricity Pool, due to be replaced by the New Electricity Trading Arrangements (NETA) in early 2001. Partly as a result, the Commission was not persuaded that it would be against the public interest for AES and British Energy to continue without the licence modification (Competition Commission, 2001). Ofgem decided to withdraw the condition, and, with the Department of Trade and Industry, was by mid-2001 consulting on a possible replacement that would apply to NETA for up to two years while it bedded down.

Several important points emerge from this episode. First, generators in Britain require a licence to operate, and that licence contains conditions governing acceptable market behaviour. Grid codes contain additional, often technical, conditions to ensure that the system operator has the requisite powers to balance electricity supply and demand and maintain system integrity and quality, but these are not sufficient to address many forms of market manipulation. Licence conditions can be modified only by agreement. If this is not possible, they are referred to the Competition Commission, which is required to determine whether the modification is required to prevent outcomes that are against the public interest.[12]

Second, the case for the MALC rested on distinctive features that favour the exercise of market power in apparently unconcentrated market structures (with Herfindahl-Hirshman indices below 1800). Specifically, electricity cannot be stored,[13] supply must be instantaneously matched to demand, transmission constraints require active systems balancing and demand is highly inelastic in the short run, over which daily price variations occur. The most obvious evidence of these distinctive characteristics is the considerable volatility over short time periods. The English pool price has moved from 17 euros/MWh to 1,700 euros/MWh over a single 24-hour period, and even more extreme price spikes have been seen in the United States. If even modest-sized generators can profitably raise prices simply by offering marginal capacity at very high prices for short periods, or in particular places, then such transient behaviour by non-dominant producers is unlikely to fall foul of normal competition law.[14]

Finally, licence conditions are important as they specify the information that must be made available to the regulator to monitor conduct. This includes details of all generating set behaviour (availability, output, bids, contract cover, for each discrete time period, typically an hour or less), as well as powers to investigate plant outages and retirement, both of which may be strategically manipulated to increase

---

[12] The public interest test is normally interpreted as a social cost-benefit test with a larger weight on consumer welfare than profits. There are proposals to replace it with a competition test, which could be interpreted as placing sole weight on long-run average consumer welfare (which may well require adequate profit incentives and rewards to ensure investment).

[13] Except as water in dams in hydro systems (including pumped storage, of which there is 2,000 MW in Britain), but the ability to withhold water in low demand periods for release at high demand periods is very limited except in a small number of countries. Even when a significant fraction of capacity is hydro (as in California), it is typically capacity-constrained at the peak.

[14] Arguably, the markets can be narrowly defined (even down to a fifteen-minute period in a constrained transmission zone) to rule out some abuses, but even this will not deal with the case of general market tightness, where a change in supply relative to total demand of 5 per cent can dramatically alter the market power of an individual generator and hence the equilibrium price.

scarcity and prices. Without such information and the authority to act quickly and effectively on their evidence, price manipulation is to be expected in tight markets. Electricity prices in the California wholesale market during the off-peak winter season January–April 2001 were ten times that in the same period in 1999, and the estimates of the additional profits that generators earned above the competitive level for the year 2000 amounted to over $8 billion (Wolak and Nordhaus, 2001). If there are no penalties or costs for this kind of behaviour, and such large rewards, privately quoted generators would be in breach of their duty to shareholders if they did not exercise their periodically considerable market power whenever possible.

At least some EU countries have liberalized their electricity industries under the requirements of the Electricity Directive, but failed to write the required information-gathering and enforcement powers into their electricity legislation. It is most unlikely that such information will be voluntarily provided. A full-scale competition inquiry with the necessary powers to request information may take months, and fail to find evidence that would stand up in court. If in addition generators are not required to hold a licence, regulators cannot follow the route open in Britain and modify the licence to prevent future abuse and to require necessary information to be routinely supplied.

The United States, with its more legalistic approach, is much clearer about the duties of regulators when liberalizing. Under the Federal Power Act 1935, the Federal Energy Regulatory Commission, FERC, has a statutory obligation to ensure that wholesale prices are 'just and reasonable'. If an electric utility wishes to sell at market-determined wholesale prices, this will be allowed only providing 'the seller (and each of its affiliates) does not have, or has adequately mitigated, market power in generation and transmission and cannot erect other barriers to entry'.[15] Even then, the authority to sell at market-determined prices can be withdrawn and replaced by regulated prices if there is 'any change in status that would reflect a departure from the characteristics the Commission has relied upon in approving market-based pricing'.[16]

FERC therefore assumes that market pricing is 'just and reasonable' so long as it is competitive. The reason for its concern to ensure that

---

[15] *Heartland Energy Services, Inc.*, 68 FERC 61,223, at 62,060 (1994), cited by Bogorad and Penn (2001).
[16] *Heartland* 68 FERC at 62,066, cited by Bogorad and Penn (2001).

prices remain competitive is that any FERC-approved form of pricing greatly restricts the competition authorities from intervening. At the same time, existing antitrust laws are relatively powerless to enforce competitive outcomes in the energy industry as 'the antitrust laws do not outlaw the mere possession of monopoly power that is the result of skill, accident, or a previous regulatory regime . . . Antitrust remedies are thus not well-suited to address problems of market power in the electric power industry that result from existing high levels of concentration in generation' (DOE, 2000: 15).

This suggests a further contrast on the two sides of the Atlantic, reflecting the prior histories of the electricity industry on the two continents. Deregulation in the United States was in principle a cautious relaxation of regulatory control over prices, with considerable awareness of the potential problems of market power. Electricity restructuring in Europe has tended to overlook issues of market power, and instead has concentrated on introducing wholesale and often retail markets in the expectation that they will be naturally competitive. The dictum of confining regulation to the natural monopolies has often been taken too literally, paying too little attention to the unnatural, or at least undesirable, monopolies in generation.

Market power and market fragmentation

The EU has adequate, arguably surplus, generation capacity, modest demand growth and access almost everywhere to gas that enables new entry by rapid-build modest-scale combined-cycle gas turbines (the least-cost choice except perhaps for hydro in favoured areas). These are ideal enabling conditions for a competitive generation market, for theory (Green and Newbery, 1992) and evidence (Newbery, 2000) alike suggest that, with a sufficient number of competing generators and adequate spare capacity, prices will be close to the competitive level. Even if generation is concentrated, provided entry is contestable (and entrants can contract with suppliers or customers), then wholesale prices should be restrained to the long-run marginal cost of generation (Newbery, 1998), even if they are too high with spare capacity.

Yet although there has been some convergence of retail prices for large customers (CEC, 2001), there are few wholesale spot markets, and those that exist are not fully arbitraged. In some cases the price differences are visible in the high auction prices for interconnection between countries, notably between Germany and the Netherlands and between France and England, although even allowing for the cost of securing interconnection there remain systematic profitable arbitrage opportunities. In other cases the interconnect auction prices are low, as between exporting Belgium and the Netherlands, although Belgian costs are well below Dutch spot prices. The absence of a wholesale market in Belgium or France, the dominance of the incumbent company in each of these countries and the fact that the Belgian electricity company, Electrabel, also owns the largest generating company in the Netherlands may explain the low interconnect auction price. The lack of wholesale markets and the presence of transmission constraints both hinder arbitrage and amplify market power in the resulting isolated markets.

Germany provides another interesting case, because the spot prices have been very low in 2000–1 (compared to the long-run marginal cost). Brunekreeft (2002) argues that the best strategy for vertically integrated generating/transmission companies wishing to deter entry is to charge avoidable cost for generation and recoup fixed costs through transmission tariffs. This strategy is possible as transmission tariffs are negotiated, and there is no sector regulator to ensure non-discriminatory access. Not surprisingly, Germany is resisting the proposed changes to the Electricity Directive. Given spare capacity, low prices are a feasible equilibrium strategy, and have the attraction of reducing the cost of buying other generating companies, allowing increasing concentration. Once the industry reaches the limits of acceptable (to the competition authorities) concentration, market power can be restored by reducing spare capacity – and plant retirements started in mid-2001.

If regulators lack the necessary competition powers, the EU electricity market risks two unattractive alternatives. At present the lack of power exchanges forces most electricity to be bought on contract – which reduces short-run market power and hedges price spikes (Newbery, 1995). Without a new directive, distribution companies retaining a domestic franchise and subject to yardstick regulation of their power contracts could provide countervailing power against generating companies. The distribution companies could contract with entrants (or even build their own capacity) to cap unreasonable price increases. However, opaque markets, lack of information and the regulatory power to enforce competitive pricing, combined with horizontal and vertical integration, may lead to the old German-style equilibrium (as described in Müller and Stahl, 1996) – safe but rather expensive.

With the new directive, the end of the franchise by 2005 is likely to encourage generators to integrate forward into supply, and risks removing the counterparties to longer-term contracts that would facilitate entry. If entry is impeded, and markets remain national and thus concentrated (because of interconnector constraints), then it will be profitable for companies to reduce the spare capacity margin, with possibly Californian consequences (worse if the regulators lack the legislative power to intervene).

Avoiding Californian-style crises

The best short-run method of supporting electricity liberalization is to rapidly increase transmission capacity (offered at efficient prices). This would increase the number of generators competing against each other, dilute market power and reduce the need for regulatory market intervention. That is difficult as it requires agreement between different regulatory regimes in each country, and because the desirable 'excess' transmission (relative to an efficient centrally managed system) is a multi-country public good. Even if successful, in the longer run, the problem is that, if demand grows and generators find it profitable to tighten capacity, high prices would be transmitted Europe-wide. To avoid that requires adequate generation capacity. Ensuring adequate capacity and contestable entry without the normal pattern of long-period commodity price swings needs good long-term contracts, possibly combined with capacity payments. Neither of these is easy in a fully liberalized market, compared to the former vertically integrated franchise model, or even the disfavoured single-buyer model. A competently regulated domestic franchise may be preferable to a fully liberalized supply market, judging from the cost–benefit analysis of Green and McDaniel (1998), and that ignored the additional contracting benefits noted here.

There are additional problems in ensuring that the benefits of capacity adequacy are captured by those providing them (the multi-country spillover problem again). Wolak (2001) recommends firm forward contracts for California (heavily dependent on out-of-state imports). As a general point, regulators should aim for capacity adequacy and maximize plant availability by ensuring maximal contract cover, and should confine any price caps to the contract market. This may require further reforms to trading arrangements, and will certainly require that regulators have adequate competition powers.

Conclusions

This chapter has argued that there is unfinished business in the areas of *regulation, restructuring,* encouraging proper *risk management* through contracting, and designing markets and regulation to ensure effective and sustainable *competition* in the services supplied over the networks. Regulators are increasingly meeting and sharing experiences, and should form a valuable constituency for further reforms of the system of regulation, so that part is well in hand. Although many are at the steep part of the learning curve, the accumulating experience of other countries ought to help in this process. Restructuring, in contrast, is far more problematic, as it requires forceful competition authorities with a clear agenda to achieve desirable structural reforms, rather than be-havioural remedies or tacit agreements on acceptable pricing. As more utilities come under private ownership, so further restructuring will be increasingly constrained by the deals that can be struck in exchange for mergers (some of which may not be desirable) or in response to the pressures applied to regulate access to essential facilities.

The main issue that may be neglected is striking the right balance between complete liberalization and ensuring adequate capacity and investment. Long-term contracts are an invaluable counterpart to spec-ulative investment in durable assets, and a retail franchise is the natural counterparty to such long-term contracts. Larger customers can either sign interruptible contracts, sign long-term contracts or take their risks in the short-term market, but domestic consumers have expectations of price stability, security of supply and quality of service that may be poorly served by a completely liberalized market. As this is one of the key proposals in the reformed energy directives, there is some urgency in assessing the balance between the benefits of competition compared with the risks of future capacity scarcity.

Finally, proactive competition policies will be necessary to resist the powerful forces for vertical and horizontal integration visible in the Union. As newly privatized utilities are freed from their domestic mar-ket, and as some state utilities can reach deep into the state's pockets to finance overseas acquisitions, so the process of acquisition and merger has gained momentum. National regulators find it difficult enough to deal with markets whose boundaries are not coincident with the national border. These problems are exacerbated where the same companies appear on both sides of that border. Greater scepticism at the concept of national champion is needed, particularly in the electricity supply industry, where economies of scale are modest beyond a certain level. Similar scepticism should be shown in the gas industry, where complex cross-holdings already compromise competitive ownership and control. Where competition is insufficient, regulators should take seriously the desirability of overinvesting in transmission and interconnection capacity, to maximize the extent of the market and the number of competitors that each company faces.

References

Bergman, L., G. Brunekreeft, C. Doyle, B.-H. von der Fehr, D. M. Newbery, M. Pollitt and P. Regibeau (1999), *A European market for electricity?*, London: Centre for Economic Policy Research.

Bogorad, C. S. and D. W. Penn (2001), 'Cost-of-service rates to market-based rates to price caps to ?!#?#!?', *Electricity Journal*, May: 61–72.

Brunekreeft, G. (2002), 'Regulation and third-party discrimination in the German electricity supply industry', *European Journal of Law and Economics*, 13: 203–220; also available at http://www.vwl.uni-freiburg.de/fakultaet/vw/lehrstuhl.html

CEC [Commission of the European Communities] (2001), *Completing the internal energy market*, Staff Working Paper, Brussels: Commission of European Communities, SEC(2001) 438.

Competition Commission (2001), *AES and British Energy*, Report 453, London: Competition Commission.

DOE [US Department of Energy] (2000), *Horizontal market power in restructured electricity markets*, US Department of Energy, Office of Economic, Electricity and Natural Gas Analysis.

Domah, P. and M. G. Pollitt (2001), 'The restructuring and privatisation of electricity distribution and supply businesses in England', *Fiscal Studies*, 22 (1): 107–146.

DRI.WEFA (2001), *Report for the European Commission Directorate General for transport and energy to determine changes after opening of the gas market in August 2000*, vol. I: *European overview*, Brussels: European Commission, http://europa.eu.imt.com/energy/en/gas single market/finalcor:vol1.pdf.

Green, R. and T. McDaniel (1998), 'Competition in electricity supply: will "1998" be worth it?', *Fiscal Studies* 19 (3): 273–293.

Green, R. and D. M. Newbery (1992), 'Competition in the British electricity spot market', *Journal of Political Economy*, 100 (5) (October): 929–953.

Müller, J. and K. Stahl (1996), 'Regulation of the market for electricity in the Federal Republic of Germany', in R. J. Gilbert and E. P. Kahn (eds.), *International comparisons of electricity regulation*, New York: Cambridge University Press, pp. 277–311.

Newbery, D. M. (1995), 'Power markets and market power', *Energy Journal*, 16 (3): 41–66.

(1998), 'Competition, contracts and entry in the electricity spot market', *Rand Journal of Economics*, 29: 726–749.

(2000), *Privatization, restructuring and regulation of network utilities*, Cambridge, MA: MIT Press.

(2002), 'Economic reform in Europe: integrating and liberalizing the market for services', *Utilities Policy*, 10: 85–97.

Newbery, D. M. and M. G. Pollitt (1997), 'The restructuring and privatisation of the CEGB – was it worth it?', *Journal of Industrial Economics*, 45 (3): 269–303.

Price C. Watts (2001), 'Heresy? The case against deregulation of electricity generation', *Electricity Journal*, May: 19–24.

Wolak, F. A. (2001), 'A comprehensive market power mitigation plan for the California electricity market', California ISO Market Surveillance Committee, 24 April, available at http://www.stanford.edu/~wolak.

Wolak, F. A. and R. Nordhaus (2001), 'Comments on "Staff recommendations on prospective market monitoring and mitigation for the California wholesale electricity market"', California ISO Market Surveillance Committee, 22 March, available at http://www.stanford.edu/~wolak.

4 | *Challenges for macroeconomic policy in EMU*

FRANCESCO GIAVAZZI

Introduction

European monetary union (EMU) has brought new challenges for macroeconomists and policy-makers alike. It has revived old issues, such as the time-honoured Balassa–Samuelson explanation of equilibrium inflation in catching-up countries, or Musgrave's analysis of capital budgets. It has also presented new questions, such as how to co-ordinate a single central bank and twelve different fiscal authorities, or which voting rules should apply in a central bank 'owned' by twelve, and possibly thirty, sovereign countries. This chapter analyses four sets of issues in the light of the experience during the first four years of monetary union:

(a) Monetary and fiscal policy co-ordination in EMU

Monetary and fiscal policies in Europe are set independently. Is this a problem? Is there a need for an explicit co-ordination of monetary and fiscal policies in EMU? Is it desirable that Ecofin and the European Central Bank (ECB) jointly decide the level of interest rates and the stance of fiscal policy? Should the twelve fiscal authorities co-ordinate their actions?

(b) Macroeconomic adjustment inside EMU

In the process leading to EMU, convergence was the name of the game. But while convergence remains important in the area of public finance, many of the interesting macroeconomic issues

---

The material presented in this chapter is based on a number of papers on the macroeconomics of EMU that I have been writing, over the past two years, with Alberto Alesina, Olivier Blanchard, Jordi Galí, Harald Uhlig, Richard Baldwin, Erik Berglöf and Mika Widgrén (Baldwin *et al.*, 2001; Alesina *et al.*, 2001a, 2001b; Blanchard and Giavazzi, 2002a, 2002b). I thank my co-authors for allowing me to use material from our joint papers freely.

within EMU today originate from macroeconomic *divergences* among member states. In Ireland, for example, the combination of high productivity growth and some overheating of the economy pushed inflation significantly above the euro area average. How should Ecofin and the ECB deal with the widening inflation differentials between high-growth countries and the core of EMU? Should such inflation differentials be a cause of concern, and if so which are the policy tools best suited to addressing the problem?

A related issue has recently received attention and has become a source of concern in EMU: should one worry about current account imbalances within the euro area? Since it was admitted into EMU, Portugal has run a current account deficit that is large by any standard, and is particularly large for a country whose current account was essentially balanced in the mid-1990s. In 2000 Portugal's current account deficit exceeded 10 per cent of GDP. Greece, the most recent member of the monetary union, is about to experience a very similar problem. To what extent are these imbalances a cause of concern?

(c) Reforming the Growth and Stability Pact

After four years of experience, the Growth and Stability Pact (GSP) is increasingly held responsible for the inability of the euro area economy to sustain demand and maintain growth. Of the various reasons why a monetary union might wish to impose fiscal rules upon its members, the pact deals with only one: the possibility that governments might be tempted to run larger budget deficits once the exchange rate and interest rates no longer respond to the fiscal actions of a single country. But there are other important issues the pact does not address. In particular, it treats low- and high-debt countries symmetrically, and thus overlooks the risks, for the single currency, that would arise if a high-debt country were to run into a roll-over crisis. More importantly, the pact exerts no pressure to reduce current government spending to make room for higher public investment and lower taxes. Should the GSP simply be scrapped?

(d) Reforming the voting rules on the ECB Council

Enlargement of EMU will soon be a reality. Under current rules, the central bank governor of each new EMU member will get a vote on the ECB's key decision-making body, the Governing Council.

Euroland's interest-setting body will thus widen from its current
eighteen members to thirty or more – clearly too many for efficient
decision-making. Reforming the voting rules prior to enlargement
is obviously easier than doing it once ten new members sit around
all wishing to get their right to vote.

Is co-ordination between Ecofin and the ECB desirable/necessary?

The ECB enjoys a considerable amount of political autonomy. It follows that monetary and fiscal policies in Europe are set independently. Is this a problem? Is there a need for explicit co-ordination
of monetary and fiscal policies in Europe in order to achieve desirable
outcomes?[1]

My answer is: no. If the monetary and fiscal authorities 'keep their
houses in order' acting on their own, there is no need for explicit co-
ordination. If the fiscal authorities deviate from 'prudent' and appropriate fiscal policies because of a variety of short-run political incentives
and constraints, then explicit co-ordination may even be counterproductive. *Formal* meetings between the monetary and fiscal authorities
designed to 'co-ordinate' policies are either unnecessary or harmful.
Informal meetings may be a useful channel of information exchange.
However, one has to weigh the benefits of this exchange of information
against the possibility that such meetings may be turned, by the fiscal
authorities, into occasions for pressuring the ECB. The participation of
the ECB president in the eurogroup meetings has to be viewed in this
context. These meetings may be useful to exchange information, but,
especially if they are sanctioned as 'formal', they may become more
than information exchange, and be counterproductive.

Co-ordination when the 'houses are in order'

Explicit co-ordination of monetary and fiscal policy is not necessary, if
the monetary and fiscal authorities (independently) follow appropriate
and prudent policies. For the monetary authority, this means keeping
inflation close to its target. Inflation targeting automatically stabilizes
output: if output is above potential, inflation will show a tendency to

[1] The issues in this section are discussed in Alesina *et al.*, 2001a.

increase, and the ECB will raise interest rates, and vice versa. As for the fiscal authorities, to 'keep their houses in order' means to maintain a cyclically adjusted balanced budget. This allows for deficits during recessions and surpluses during expansions because of automatic stabilizers.

Under these circumstances, there is not much that explicit monetary and fiscal policy co-ordination can achieve. Fiscal authorities in different countries remain free to tailor policies to their country's preferences. These policies will influence the size of government, the allocation between public and private consumption and investment, and the level of taxation and redistribution. All of these choices will affect the composition of output, and some of them the level of potential output. None of them require 'co-ordination' with a central bank pursuing a policy of inflation targeting, and thus the goal of maintaining the euroland level of output close to potential.

A specific example helps to clarify this point. In the current European macroeconomic environment, fiscal authorities are preoccupied that their inability to use fiscal policy actively (because of the constraints imposed by the GSP) may worsen the economic slowdown. Co-ordination, it is argued, is desirable and should take the form of an agreement between the ECB and the finance ministers, resulting in an unchanged fiscal stance combined with easier money. In fact, explicit co-ordination is not necessary. If the ECB followed an 'inflation-targeting' approach, then if the absence of fiscal stimulus were to generate a downturn the effect of the latter on the output gap, and thus on inflation, would automatically trigger a monetary policy response in the direction of 'easing'. If the monetary policy rule is clearly understood by the fiscal authorities – an important 'if', as discussed below – there is no reason why they should be concerned, and thus no reason to believe that explicit co-ordination would produce a better outcome. A good example was the mix achieved – without formal co-ordination – at the end of 2002: lower interest rates, while fiscal authorities were trying to balance their cyclically adjusted budgets.

One may argue that a need for co-ordination emerges because of the timing of policy actions. Consider the case in which the fiscal authorities wished to cut the deficit, but refrained from doing so, worrying that the ECB might not step in with easy money. That is, the fiscal authorities may postpone deficit reduction, waiting for the ECB to 'ease', while the latter will lower rates only if and when a fiscally induced downturn materializes. However, even this timing issue is not a real problem and does not require explicit co-ordination.

First, the fiscal authorities (and the public) should be sure that inflation targeting automatically implies an ECB intervention in case of a fall of output below potential. Second, fiscal policy packages, i.e., government budgets, are approved several months in advance of their implementation. Monetary policy changes, on the other hand, can be decided much more swiftly and more often. Third, the approval and implementation of fiscal policy is subject to a considerable level of political uncertainty. Suppose that the finance ministers sincerely 'promise' a fiscal tightening with the next budget, and assume that the ECB 'co-ordinates' and, in anticipation of the fiscal manoeuvre, reduces interest rates. If the political climate changes, and the fiscal manoeuvre is abandoned, then the monetary and fiscal package is 'wrong', namely it is overexpansionary. In addition, the monetary loosening may actually provide a temporary improvement of the non-cyclically adjusted fiscal balance through lower interest rates and growth, reducing the incentives for the discretionary fiscal tightening.

The political economy of co-ordination

Even the best-intentioned finance ministers are subject to a very large amount of political constraints, from electoral concerns, to the obligation to 'strike deals' with opposition parties, to the necessity of favouring certain constituencies, such as public sector unions and so forth.

The complex political 'game' that leads to the formulation of fiscal policy often brings about departures from optimal and prudent policies. In this situation, active co-ordination with the monetary authority could make matters worse. On the contrary, lack of explicit co-ordination may help create incentives for the fiscal authorities to act more in line with optimality principles. The GSP is, in fact, motivated by the fear that, without this constraint, fiscal authorities may not keep prudent budgets. Without any preoccupation that politics may distort fiscal policy, there would be no need for a stability pact.

The typical case is one in which the fiscal authority wants to overexpand (or not tighten enough). In these situations it would pressure the ECB to 'accommodate', since sticking to inflation targeting would lead to a restrictive monetary policy, high interest rates and a real appreciation of the exchange rate. If the 'co-ordination' does not occur, the fiscal authority would invoke the lack of co-ordination of policies (expansionary fiscal, contractionary monetary) as the culprit for the ensuing downturn. However, 'co-ordination' in this scenario means that the central bank should abandon the normal inflation targeting. This would not be a good solution, as it simply postpones the costs of a recession needed to eradicate inflation.

The need for transparent inflation targeting

The argument against explicit co-ordination assumes that the fiscal authorities can be perfectly sure about the reaction of the ECB, following various fiscal choices, so that they may incorporate this reaction into their plans. Knowing that an overly expansionary fiscal policy would not be accommodated would restrain them; knowing that the possible downturn created by a fiscal consolidation would induce a loosening of monetary policy would weaken the political opposition to budget cuts. This is one of the benefits of clearly stated monetary rules.

The bottom line is that any degree of uncertainty about the response of the ECB to a move of the fiscal authorities would justify their call for taking decisions jointly, i.e., for formal co-ordination. The ECB would then have a hard time explaining why it does not wish to take part in such exercises.

During its first four years, the ECB has not followed a strict inflation-targeting rule. Its strategy has been more elaborate and involves two 'pillars', inflation and money growth. Does this justify 'co-ordination' with fiscal authorities? The answer is, again, no. The fact that ECB policies leave more room for discretion than a simple 'inflation-targeting' rule, on balance makes co-ordination even less desirable. In fact, to the extent that monetary policy does not follow a simple rule, the fiscal authorities may have more 'room to manoeuvre' in putting pressure on the ECB. I see this as a rather strong argument in favour of the rapid adoption of an inflation-targeting rule.

Meetings between the ECB and the eurogroup

The Nice Treaty has opened the road for the formal participation of the ECB in the meetings of the eurogroup. The Treaty provides a new institutional framework which could allow formal co-ordination between monetary and fiscal policy inside EMU. The procedures for 'reinforced co-operation' make it possible to formalize the dialogue, which has so far been informal, and which takes place among the twelve finance ministers, and between them and the president of the ECB in the so-called eurogroup. (The ECB, in the October 2000 *Bulletin*, said that it considers such a dialogue useful.)

The previous discussion on the pros and cons of co-ordination of monetary and fiscal policy raises considerable concerns about these meetings. They can certainly serve as a forum for the exchange of information, even though to the extent that information should be publicly available exchanging it may not require closed-door meetings at the highest level. Nevertheless, meetings among well-intentioned policy-makers may serve useful purposes.

As argued above, however, one cannot assume that fiscal authorities are always free from political incentives that lead them to deviate from policy-making with a long-term view. In this case the danger of these meetings is that they can provide an officially sanctioned forum for the fiscal authorities to put pressure on the ECB. Whether or not the latter might be influenced would depend, in part, on the personalities involved. In some cases the ECB might be negatively affected. In other cases, the influence of the ECB may lead to an improvement of the fiscal stance.

The potential danger of these meetings obviously increases with their formality. The United States provides an interesting comparison. The weekly breakfast meeting between the chairman of the Federal Reserve Board and the secretary of the Treasury is very informal and does not seem to compromise the degree of independence of the Fed. If these meetings assumed a much more formal format, and were officially sanctioned by law, they might take on a very different character, and they might affect the perceived degree of independence of the Fed.

Participation of the ECB in formal meetings of the eurogroup would make such encounters very different from the informal breakfast, US-style. But formality would be hard to avoid given the size of these meetings, involving not one but twelve ministers. Overall, my judgement is that the potential benefits of these formal meetings are inferior to the risks they entail.

Multiple fiscal authorities

Thus far I have ignored the fact that in EMU there are twelve fiscal authorities, rather than one. Should these twelve finance ministers co-ordinate their policies? And what are the implications for the monetary-fiscal policy mix? Again, if the fiscal authorities follow 'optimal' fiscal policies, there is no need for co-ordination.[2] Note that given non-perfectly synchronized business cycles, the budgets of the twelve countries would also not be synchronized, and it would be a mistake to make surpluses/deficits identical for all countries at every point in time.

An interesting case, however, is the following. Suppose that several well-intentioned finance ministers want to reduce deficits and retire excessive debt, inherited from the past. The potential costs of a fiscal contraction for each country acting alone may be higher than those incurred by a co-ordinated move. If a fiscal authority were to act alone, and if the fiscal contraction caused a nation-specific downturn, the ECB would not step in, since the ECB targets euroland, not any specific country. In this case co-ordination among the twelve would make sense.

The benefits of co-ordination among the twelve are less clear if the fiscal authorities are motivated by short-term political goals. Suppose that the fiscal authorities want to overexpand for short-term political gains. If a country acted alone, it would create inflation and real exchange-rate appreciation. But if the twelve did it together, the ECB would step in and tighten monetary policy to prevent an acceleration of inflation, if the latter materialized. Which of the two scenarios is more costly for the country with a loose fiscal policy is unclear. If it is more costly to act alone, then co-ordination reduces the cost of an incorrect policy action, and may thus make it more attractive.

Whether or not the twelve fiscal authorities co-ordinate with each other also has implications for the relationship with the ECB. If the fiscal authorities are 'well intentioned' then, although co-ordination remains unnecessary, the meeting with the ECB may indeed provide

---

[2] By 'fiscal policy' I mean here the aggregate budget position. I ignore the issue of the co-ordination of tax systems. Regardless of whether the latter is desirable or not, in any case it would entail rewriting legislation, not a day-to-day co-ordination of policy decisions, which is the topic under consideration here.

a useful exchange of views and information. If fiscal authorities co-ordinate on the 'wrong' policies, then, acting as a 'united front', they may increase the pressure on the ECB to deviate from inflation target-ing.

Should inflation divergences within the euro area be a source of concern?

In a number of countries, especially those where inflation has started increasing faster than the euro zone average, the argument has been made that this higher inflation is an equilibrium phenomenon, and thus nothing to worry about.[3] Higher inflation, the argument goes, does not come about because output exceeds potential: it simply reflects the adjustment of relative prices naturally associated with growth, and is known as the Balassa–Samuelson effect.

There is little question that, where the argument has been made, it has been in part self-serving, coming from a desire to 'justify' what would otherwise be perceived as a sin, namely inflation higher than the euro zone average. But, whatever the confused motivation, the argument is based on solid theoretical grounds. The point is to have an idea of how large the Balassa–Samuelson effect could be, and whether it is enough to explain the inflation differentials observable across the members of EMU.

Equilibrium inflation rates and the Balassa–Samuelson effect

Consider an economy with both tradable and non-tradable goods. Sup-pose that productivity growth is faster in the tradable than in the non-tradable sector – which it typically is. Productivity growth, together with a given world price for tradables, implies a steady increase in the real wage in terms of tradables (assuming that profits are tied down by the world real interest rate and thus cannot change). The increases in the real wage and lower productivity growth in non-tradables com-bine to imply an increase in the relative price of non-tradables. This is known as the Balassa–Samuelson effect. The argument is particularly relevant for emerging countries, countries which are catching up fast. In these countries, the relative price of non-tradables must increase,

---

[3] The issues in this section are discussed in Alesina *et al.*, 2001a.

leading to a steady increase in the relative price level or, equivalently, to higher inflation.

How large is this effect likely to be for euro zone countries? The study by De Gregorio and Wolff (1994) provides a good starting point. Using data from fourteen OECD countries from 1970 to 1985, they regress real exchange rates for each country for each year on a country dummy, total factor productivity growth in tradables relative to non-tradables, an index of terms of trade and the ratio of government spending to output. They obtain the following regression results:

$$\Delta \log(P/eP^*) = .197\Delta \log(a_T/a_N) + .485\Delta \log(P_X/P_M)$$
$$+ 3.458\Delta \log(G/Y),$$

where e, P^* and P are the nominal exchange rate, the world price level and the domestic price level respectively, a_T and a_N are total factor productivity growth rates in the tradable and non-tradable sectors respectively, P_X and P_M are the price of exports and imports respectively and G/Y is the ratio of government spending (presumably mostly on non-traded goods and services, hence the positive sign) to GDP.

The relevant term here is the first, which gives the effects of relative productivity growth in the tradable and non-tradable sectors on the relative price level. I shall use it to get a sense of the likely magnitude of the Balassa–Samuelson effect in two specific cases, those of Ireland and Spain.

Ireland

A Solow growth decomposition suggests that, from 1995 to 2000, annual total factor productivity growth (tfp) for the Irish economy as a whole was around 4.3 per cent. To get an upper bound, assume (and this is surely excessive) that tfp growth has been 8 per cent in the tradable sector, and 2 per cent in the non-tradable sector. Assume, and this is again excessive, that, in the rest of euroland, there was no difference between tfp growth in the tradable and the non-tradable sectors. This, then, would translate into an increase of 8 per cent times .197 or about 1.5 per cent a year more inflation in Ireland than in euroland. This generous upper bound is still quite small considering that over the first two years of EMU Irish inflation has been on average 2.5 percentage points higher than the euroland rate.

Spain

The Balassa–Samuelson effect has been invoked in Spain, though it is hard to see how the effect can be quantitatively relevant. Recent output growth in Spain has come mostly from the decrease in unemployment, not from productivity growth, which has been very low, about 1 per cent,[4] far below the euroland average. This suggests that, if anything, the Balassa–Samuelson effect is going the wrong way for Spain.

How to adjust when adjustment is needed?

Let us now move away from the Balassa–Samuelson case. Suppose output in a euro country starts exceeding potential output, and inflation starts increasing. The country has two ways of adjusting: either by letting inflation increase above the euroland average, leading to appreciation and a decrease in foreign demand, or by using fiscal policy, to decrease domestic demand instead. Neither way is *a priori* good or bad. Which one is appropriate depends on external and internal conditions. To pursue this point, let us use a conventional textbook model, some simple algebra and an associated diagram. Let the condition for equilibrium in the goods market (IS) be given by:

$$\text{IS:} \quad y = a(y, g) + nx(\varepsilon, y)$$

where y is output, a(.,.) is the sum of consumption, investment and government spending, and is assumed to be a function of output and some index of fiscal policy, g, with $a_y > 0$ and $a_g > 0$; nx(.,.) is net exports, assumed to be a function of the real exchange rate, ε, and output, with $nx_\varepsilon > 0$ (an increase in ε is a real depreciation, and improves net exports), and $nx_y < 0$ (an increase in output increases imports, reducing net exports).

Internal balance requires $y = y^*$ where y^* is equilibrium output. External balance requires balanced trade, $nx(\varepsilon,y) = 0$.

---

[4] One may wonder whether this surprisingly low number is not in part the result of mismeasurement. A careful study by Estrada and Lopez-Salido (2001) suggests that this is not the case. It finds a rate of total factor productivity growth equal to 1.8 per cent for the period 1980–95 for the Spanish economy as a whole, and to 1.9 per cent for manufacturing. The study also shows clear evidence of a decrease in both rates of growth in the 1990s.

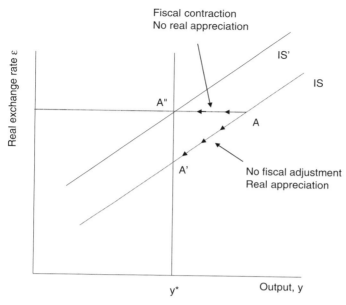

Figure 4.1 Adjustment of an overheating economy

Finally, through a conventional Phillips curve, assume that internal imbalance leads to an *increase* in inflation and thus to *faster* real appreciation:

$$\Delta^2\varepsilon = -\Delta\pi = -f(y - y^*).$$

These relations are plotted in figure 4.1, with the real exchange rate on the vertical axis, and output on the horizontal axis. The IS relation is drawn for a given value of g, and is upward-sloping: a depreciation leads to an increase in equilibrium output. The internal balance equation is vertical at $y = y^*$. To the right of y^*, the real exchange rate appreciates, and the economy moves down along the IS curve. To the left of y^*, the real exchange rate depreciates, and the economy moves up along the IS curve.

Now suppose that the economy is overheating, at point A. One option is to let the economy run its course unhindered, with inflation leading to appreciation, and a return of the economy to point A'. Another is to rely on fiscal contraction, to shift the IS curve to IS', leading the economy to rest at point A''. In both cases, the economy

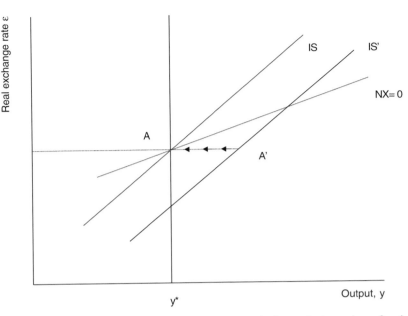

Figure 4.2 Adjusting to an increase in internal demand through a fiscal contraction

eventually returns to the same level of equilibrium output, y^*. What differs is the real exchange rate, and thus the composition of demand, internal versus external. The more use of fiscal contraction, the smaller the real appreciation, the more favourable the external balance.

What instrument should the government use? This obviously depends on the source of overheating: internal or external demand. Turn to figure 4.2. In addition to the IS locus, draw the locus along which there is external balance, $NX = 0$. The locus is upward-sloping: an increase in output deteriorates the trade balance, requiring a depreciation, i.e., an increase in ε. It is flatter than the IS. (To see this, start from the point on the IS where there is external balance, and move up along the IS. As, by assumption, the domestic marginal propensity to spend is less than one, the difference must be made up by an improvement in the trade position. Thus, we move from balance to surplus. Put another way, an appreciation is needed to re-establish external balance: the $NX = 0$ locus is below the IS.)

Assume that, initially, the economy is at point A, with both internal and external balance. Now assume that internal demand shifts up.

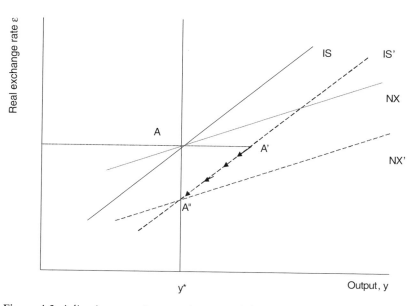

Figure 4.3 Adjusting to an increase in external demand through inflation and real appreciation

The IS curve shifts to the right to IS′, while the NX = 0 locus remains unchanged. The economy is now at A′, with higher output and a trade deficit. What is required in this case is clearly the use of fiscal policy, a fiscal contraction which shifts the IS curve back to its original position, and returns the economy to both internal and external balance.

The case where the source of the shock is external demand instead is represented in figure 4.3. For a given value of y, the shift in external demand shifts the NX locus down from NX to NX′: external balance requires an appreciation. And, for a given y, the shift in IS is the same as the shift in NX. The effect of the shift is to take the economy to A′, with higher output and a trade surplus. In this case, the appropriate policy is clearly not to use fiscal policy, and let the economy adjust along the new IS curve, IS′, back to A″. At A″, the economy achieves both external and internal balance. Put another way, the right response to the increase in external demand is to let the relative price of domestic goods increase so as to decrease demand and return output to normal. This increase in the relative price, and the associated increase in real income, is achieved by letting inflation exceed euro zone inflation for some time.

This analysis is too simple in many ways. With Ireland and Spain in mind, let us mention a few of these.

External balance, i.e., trade or current account balance, may well not be the right target for an economy, in particular for an economy with a high underlying rate of growth, such as Ireland. To the extent that profit opportunities are present and lead to a high investment rate, it may well be best for the economy to run current account deficits now, in anticipation of current account surpluses in the future. In this case, inflation may well be the right instrument, even if it leads to a current account deficit at equilibrium output levels.

Whether to use fiscal policy and how to choose the appropriate budget position must clearly depend on the initial fiscal situation, *vis à vis* both the deficit and the level of debt. If debt is still high, or if spending is anticipated to be higher in the future, a more conservative fiscal policy is then appropriate, and with it more of a focus on fiscal contraction than on inflation as the method of adjustment. On the contrary, if debt is falling, the budget shows a surplus, and public investment, for instance in infrastructure, offers the prospect of hefty social returns, the conclusion may then be the opposite: a temporary fiscal expansion with the adjustment falling entirely on an accelerated inflation differential.

Finally, the use of each of the two tools has its own complex dynamics.

Adjusting through inflation may not be so easy. Given inflation inertia, there is clearly the risk of achieving too large a real appreciation, of reducing competitiveness by too much. Having inflation return to the euroland level just when the real exchange rate is at the right level is at best a delicate exercise. On the other side, with a common nominal interest rate throughout EMU, a country with higher inflation will have a lower real interest rate: this will expand domestic demand, working against the real appreciation. Eventually, however, the real appreciation will dominate, since the fall in the real interest rate is proportional to the inflation differential, while the real exchange rate keeps appreciating at the rate of the inflation differential.

Using fiscal policy is not so easy either. Leaving aside automatic stabilizers, decision and implementation lags make it hard to get the timing right, and the lesson of history is that the fiscal policy response often comes too late.

But, leaving these complications aside, the analysis yields a simple but important implication. Domestic inflation, which is better thought of as an increase in the relative price of domestic goods, may well be a desirable part of the adjustment process. The more external demand is the source of overheating, the more inflation is the natural instrument to return the economy to sustainable output levels. In that context, it should be not denied or dismissed (by invoking the Balassa–Samuelson effect), not put off the table from the start, but accepted and explained.

Should current account imbalances within the euro area be a source of concern?

In 2000–1, the current account deficit of Portugal reached 10 per cent of GDP, up from 2.3 per cent at the start of the 1990s.[5] Forecasts are for these deficits to continue in the 8–9 per cent range for the indefinite future. Greece is not far behind. Its current account deficit in 2000–1 was equal to 6–7 per cent of GDP, up from 1.2 per cent in the early 1990s and, again, the forecasts are for deficits to remain high, in the 5–6 per cent range.

This is not the first time that some of the small member countries of the European Union have run large current account deficits. In the early 1980s, Portugal, for example, ran deficits in excess of 10 per cent of GDP. But these deficits had a very different flavour: Portugal then was still reeling from its 1975 revolution, from the loss of its colonies and from the second oil shock; the government was running a large budget deficit, in excess of 16 per cent of GDP. The current account deficits were widely perceived as unsustainable, and indeed they turned out to be: between 1980 and 1987, the escudo was devalued by 60 per cent, and the current account deficit eliminated. In contrast, Portugal today is not suffering from large adverse shocks; the official budget deficit has been reduced since the early 1990s (although with some signs of relapse in 2002, as current estimates imply that Portugal may exceed the limits imposed by the GSP), and financial markets show no sign of worry.

The fact that Portugal and Greece are each members of both the European Union and the euro area, and, in each case, are the poorest members, suggests a natural explanation for these current account deficits. They are exactly what theory suggests can and should happen when countries become more closely linked in goods and financial

[5] The issues in this section are discussed in Blanchard and Giavazzi, 2002a.

markets. To the extent that they are the countries with higher rates of return, poor countries should see an increase in investment. And to the extent that they are the countries with higher growth prospects, they should also see a decrease in saving. Thus, on both counts, poor countries should run larger current account deficits. Symmetrically, richer countries should run larger current account surpluses.

Blanchard and Giavazzi (2002a) investigate whether this hypothesis indeed fits the facts. They conclude that it does, with saving rather than investment as the main channel through which integration affects current account balances. Using panel data evidence from the OECD since 1975, the paper documents that the recent evolution of Portugal and Greece is indeed part of a more general evolution: the dispersion of current account positions has steadily increased since the early 1990s. And current account positions have become increasingly related to the level of output per capita of the country. This evolution is visible within the OECD as a whole, but is stronger within the European Union, and stronger still within the euro area. The channel appears to be primarily through a decrease in saving – typically private saving – rather than through an increase in investment.

To give a visual impression of these findings, figure 4.4 shows a set of scatterplots of the time average of the ratio of the current account deficit to GDP against the time average of output per capita, for two subperiods, 1985–93 and 1994–2000, for different groups of countries. Output per capita is constructed as GDP per capita in 1985 dollars correcting for changes in purchasing power, using the data from Heston and Summers up to 1992, and extrapolated using real GDP growth rates thereafter. The country groups are:

- 'OECD minus', i.e., all OECD countries except Mexico, Turkey, Korea, Central European countries (the Czech Republic, Slovakia, Hungary and Poland) and Luxembourg – twenty-two countries in all;
- 'European Union', the group of European Union countries, excluding Luxembourg, so fourteen countries in all;
- 'euro area', or euro for short, the countries now in the euro area, minus Luxembourg, so eleven countries in all (Greece, which joined in 2001, is included throughout);
- 'euro minus', the set of countries in the euro area, minus Portugal and Greece, nine countries in all. The reason for looking at this subgroup is simply to see whether the results for the euro area are due to these two countries or hold even in the rest of the Euro area.

Figure 4.4 and associated regressions (regression lines are shown in each panel) have two striking features:

- there is a substantial strengthening of the relation between the current account and output per capita from the first to the second subsample. Except for the euro area, the regression coefficient is typically insignificant for 1985–93; it becomes much larger and very significant in 1994–2000; and
- the increase is stronger for the EU than for the OECD as a whole, and stronger for the euro area than for the EU (although the difference between EU and the euro area is neither statistically nor economically significant).

Both features are very much consistent with the idea that integration is an important factor behind current account evolutions. Integration was higher to start with within the EU or the euro area, and has continued at a higher pace.

The visual impression from figure 4.4 is confirmed by the statistical analysis in Blanchard and Giavazzi (2002a), in which standard current account panel regressions are run with income per capita and a set of controls as explanatory variables.

Is benign neglect the optimal policy response?

So far, the attitude of both the European Commission and the European Central Bank *vis à vis* the Portuguese and Greek current account deficits has been one of benign neglect. That attitude is the same as that prevailing in the United States towards state deficits. Current account deficits of individual states are not even recorded, much less worried about. Is the same attitude justified for the countries of the euro area? Let us briefly review what theory tells us:

- If these current account deficits had their origin in large fiscal deficits, then issues of intergenerational distribution would obviously arise. Higher government debt would mean higher taxes in the future, and thus a higher burden on future generations. But, in this case, the issue is moot: as we have seen, the current account deficits have their origin in private saving and private investment. The consumers who are taking mortgages in Portugal are the ones who will have to repay them, not future generations. They may be too optimistic about future income prospects, but we do not typically think of this as a reason for macro policy intervention.

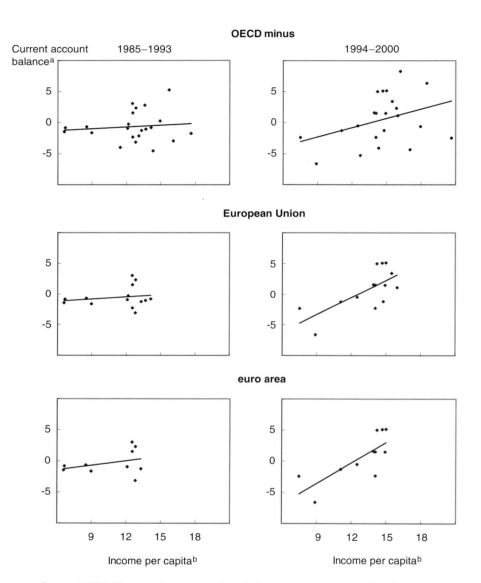

Source: AMECO (European Commission's Annual Macroeconomic Database of the Directorate General for Economic and Financial Affairs) and data from Alan Heston and Robert Summers, Penn World Tables (pwt.econ.upenn.edu).
a. Current account balances are expressed as a percentage of GDP.
b. Values are in thousands of 1985 dollars at purchasing power parity.

Figure 4.4 Average current account balances and income per capita, selected country groups, 1985–2000

- Even so, ever since the work of Diamond (1965) on overlapping generation economies, we know that, in a closed economy, individual saving decisions may be privately optimal, but still lead either to an inefficient aggregate outcome (in the case of dynamic inefficiency), or to one with unappealing implications in terms of intergenerational distribution: if current consumers save little, the capital stock will be smaller, and so will the income of future generations. Thus, in a closed economy, low private saving may well justify government intervention on behalf of future generations, for example in the form of higher public saving.

- This last argument becomes weaker, however, when the economy is open (see Buiter (1981) for an analysis of the overlapping generation model in an open economy). Consider, for example, the limiting case in which the economy is open and fully integrated in world financial markets, and the elasticity of demand for domestic goods is infinite – so we are, in effect, in a 'one-good world'. Then, the issue of generational redistribution becomes irrelevant. Saving decisions in the country have no effect on investment in the country, and thus have no effect on future output and no effect on the income of future generations. The very integration which leads to larger current account deficits also reduces their generational distribution implications.

- This limiting case is too strong, however. Even euro area countries are short of being fully integrated, and surely face downward-sloping demand for their goods. And so, to the extent that large current account deficits today lead to the need for trade surpluses in the future, they also lead to the need for low relative prices for domestic goods in the future, and so to lower income (in terms of consumption) for future generations. In this case, the legacy of high current account deficits is not low capital, but their adverse effect on future terms of trade. This provides an argument for higher public saving today; but the argument seems empirically weaker than the standard closed economy capital accumulation argument.

Now turn to implications for fiscal policy (the Greek or Portuguese governments obviously have no control over euro zone monetary policy, and because of the symmetry between current account surpluses and deficits across countries in the euro area, the ECB has no reason to respond by changing monetary policy):

- If the governments of Portugal and Greece do not change their fiscal stance, the shifts in saving and investment in response to integration will lead to output in excess of its natural level. This in turn will lead to higher inflation than in the rest of the euro area, and thus eventually will generate the required appreciation.

- If those governments decide instead to maintain output at its natural level, say through higher public saving, they will, by implication, reduce the current account deficit. Under the assumption that the marginal propensity to import is the same for all types of spending (consumption, investment, government), the use of fiscal policy to maintain output at its natural level will imply eliminating the current account deficit altogether.

- Only a formal quantitative model can tell us exactly what fiscal policy should be in this case. But it is surely not to fully offset the increase in private spending so as to maintain output at its natural level. This would have the implication of largely or fully eliminating the current account deficit, thus losing one of the main benefits of economic integration, namely the ability to intertemporally reallocate consumption and investment. So, while benign neglect may not be optimal, it appears, at least for those deficits, to be a reasonable course of action.

Should euro area members follow the example of US states and stop collecting current account statistics? There are at least three reasons for caution. The fact that European product markets are not yet fully integrated implies that the changes in relative prices required to service or repay the debt remain larger than in the United States: for this reason, policy-makers will want to know how much foreign debt a country is accumulating. Second, the potential output costs of adjusting relative prices – through a recession reducing the inflation rate below the EU inflation rate – constitute another reason to worry about the level of foreign debt. Finally, euro fiscal rules may prove weaker than those that stop US states from running large budget deficits: in such a situation, knowing the effect of the budget deficit on the current account would certainly be valuable.

Improving the Growth and Stability Pact through a proper accounting of public investment

The GSP is increasingly held responsible for the inability of the euro area economy to sustain demand and maintain growth – a concern that extends beyond Europe since the United States has stopped providing growth for the world economy.

There are a number of proposals to improve the GSP – from simply scrapping it, to applying it to cyclically adjusted, rather than actual budget figures.

Blanchard and Giavazzi (2002b) discuss one amendment to the GSP which has three desirable characteristics:

- it is compatible with the European treaties, and thus easy to implement;
- it corrects an obvious mistake in the way the GSP was written; and
- it would help in the current slowdown.

The amendment I propose is separate, and more explicit and transparent: treatment of investment expenditures. No private company attributes to a single year's accounts the entire cost of an investment project whose benefits will come over a long period of time. Investment implies future returns: its cost should thus be distributed over time, as those returns accrue. Amortization of investment expenditures by governments is not allowed by the GSP, although the Treaty does not prevent it.

The paper also discusses how to properly account for public investment, and how to treat it under GSP rules. If, as Article 104.3 of the Treaty allows, the current rules of the GSP were applied to a budget for which the treatment of investment expenditures was done properly – which means applying the rules of the GSP to the budget inclusive of nominal interest payments and of capital depreciation, but excluding net investment – over time the debt–GDP ratio would converge on the ratio of public capital to GDP. Eventually public debt will be, on average, equal to public capital. Deviations from that level will serve the purpose of providing the budget with enough flexibility to deal with cyclical fluctuations in output, and will fluctuate around zero.

A correct accounting of public investment would have three advantages.

- It would remove financial constraints on public investment. This is important in the euro area, for two reasons. First, gross public investment in the twelve EMU countries has been on a downward path since the mid-1970s, falling, as a share of GDP, from 4 per cent in the early 1970s to less than 2.5 per cent in 1998. In particular public investment fell by 0.8 percentage points during the run-up to the euro (1993–7). Today average gross investment is 2.4 per cent of

GDP, but net investment is probably close to zero in Germany, Italy, Belgium and Austria. Second, the enlargement of the EU opens up opportunities for valuable public investment projects: this is certainly true for the accession countries, but in the existing EU member states investment opportunities will also widen – for instance, because the geographic size of EU markets will increase.

- It would introduce more transparency in the budget. The inability to treat investment separately has created, in some countries, the incentive to shift borrowing off-budget. Italy, for instance, has recently set up an agency fully owned by the government but not consolidated in the government accounts, whose purpose is to finance and run public investment projects, borrowing on the market. There is nothing wrong with investment agencies as such: the separation of the 'current' budget from the 'capital' budget has a time-honoured tradition in public finance (Musgrave, 1939). What is inappropriate is the lack of transparency. The accounts of these agencies, for instance, make no distinction between gross and net investment, and thus fail to recognize that depreciation of public capital is equivalent to current expenditure and should be treated as such in the consolidated government accounts. The agencies have no clear limits on the amount they can borrow. The bonds they issue are guaranteed by the government, but such guarantees are not recorded in the government books. Thus the debt they issue is not considered as part of the public debt. The European Commission has questioned these guarantees, arguing that they are often equivalent to state aid. There certainly are instances – and the recent capital injection by the Kreditanstalt für Wiederaufbau into a German private communications company is one example – when these agencies engage in state aid. But this is not the case in general: subsidizing public projects whose social return exceeds their financial return is one of the reasons governments exist. The agencies should receive a transfer from the central government which reflects the fact that public projects have a financial return, net of capital depreciation, which may be less than the market return. They should be allowed to borrow on the market an amount equal to their net investment in new public projects. Running an agency properly raises an incentive problem, because whatever financial return the agency extracts from its projects, the central budget will make up for the difference. The contract between the agency's manager and the central government should thus be carefully designed.

- Excluding net public investment from the definition of the budget that is relevant for the GSP would also help in the short run. Consider Germany, for instance, one of the countries where a change in the rules would apparently not matter, since net public investment today is essentially zero. With the current interpretation of the GSP, and assuming that German output is below potential by an amount large enough to justify the entire use of the 3 per cent band – which is probably the case – Germany would need to cut the deficit by at least 0.8 per cent of GDP. The modified rule also requires fiscal action, but of a very different type. To satisfy the rule, the German government would have to replace at least 0.8 per cent of GDP of current expenditure with an equivalent amount of public investment. The effect on aggregate demand is very different under the two rules.

Reforming the voting rules on the Council of the ECB

The economies of the new EMU members will more closely resemble that of Ireland than that of Germany or other core euroland nations. They are small and marked by high growth and high structural inflation. The Governing Council thus risks becoming divided between a dozen or more high-growth–high-inflation 'Irelands' and a handful of 'core' nations, with the 'Irelands' having enough votes to set interest rates though they account for only 20 per cent of euroland output.

Enlargement will weaken the relative power of the body's leader, namely the president and Executive Board. Enlargement without reform would also create an opportunity for coalitions formed by EMU members with less-synchronized economies to win the day, setting interest rates for the whole area while representing only about 20 per cent of the euroland's GDP. Finally, enlargement might induce a status quo bias, making it more difficult to react to significant changes in the macroeconomic climate.

There are three leading contenders for reforming the Governing Council's decision-making rules: rotation, representation and delegation. Both rotation and representation have shortcomings: neither is likely to lead to appropriate monetary policy decisions. Best practice in central banking strongly argues in favour of delegation to an independent committee. Unfortunately, the ECB seems to be moving in the direction of rotation, simply because this is the least politically difficult solution. Why would delegation be better, and how can it be made palatable to the member countries?

The EU has clear supranational executive power in two areas only: competition policy and monetary policy. In the case of competition policy, the power is delegated to a committee – the Commission – and decisions are made without formal consultation with either the Council of Ministers or EU members in general. Delegating interest-rate decisions to a committee is thus consistent both with best practice in central banking and with current EU practice.

The committee in charge of monetary policy decisions should include the six members of the Executive Board (EB) plus a few non-executive members. My suggested membership of such a committee is eleven, six EB members plus five non-executive members.

Removing national central bank governors from the Governing Council, however, has a cost. Governors have credibility in the eyes of their fellow citizens. They are typically viewed as eminent citizens in touch with national sensitivities. Cutting them out of the ECB process entirely might seriously weaken the ECB's accountability and political acceptability. To redress this, and ensure that the full range of monetary conditions have a voice, I suggest that the views of central bank governors could still enter the process but only as information that Committee members use to reach their decision. The central bank governors would continue to be part of the Governing Council, but this would become, as far as monetary policy decisions are concerned, a consultative body, one that ensures that the governors can continue to function in the role of national 'listening posts'.

Baldwin *et al.* (2001) argue that, as a matter of urgent concern, the ECB should formulate a response to this challenge. The urgency stems from the fact that even medium-term challenges may have immediate effect when they are predictable. Every day, financial markets must set prices for ten-year euro debt instruments with an eye to future monetary policy, which, ultimately, depends on the ECB's decision-making structure. It is therefore important to provide clear indications that the ECB's numbers problem will be solved.

Summary

In summary, is there a need for an explicit co-ordination of monetary and fiscal policies in EMU? No. If the monetary and fiscal authorities 'keep their houses in order', there is no need for explicit co-ordination. If the fiscal authorities deviate from 'prudent' fiscal policies because of a variety of short-run political incentives and constraints, then explicit co-ordination may even be counterproductive. This conclusion carries an important caveat. Any degree of uncertainty about the response of monetary policy to a move of the fiscal authorities would justify their call for taking decisions jointly, i.e., for formal co-ordination. The ECB would then have a hard time explaining why it does not wish to take part in such exercises. In other words, the ECB's stubborn insistence on the 'two pillars' strategy may produce bad monetary policy decisions as well as an undesirable policy mix.

Inflation differentials should not be demonized. In a common currency area inflation differentials are the mechanism for adjusting real exchange rates, when adjustment is needed. For a country belonging to a currency union, having higher inflation than the average may thus be entirely appropriate. After having convinced citizens that inflation is bad, governments and the ECB must now go to step two, and explain that temporary inflation differentials can be desirable, leading to higher real income and the proper macroeconomic adjustment.

The current account deficits that have emerged in the lower-income countries of the euro area are indicative of important and good developments. In economies that are integrating into the euro area, and start from a level of income below the average, using fiscal policy to stop a current account deficit from emerging would amount to losing one of the main benefits of economic integration, namely the ability to intertemporally reallocate consumption and investment. So, while benign neglect may not be optimal, it appears, at least for those deficits, to be a reasonable course of action.

Amending the Growth and Stability Pact to allow for the separate, and more explicit and transparent, treatment of investment expenditures has three desirable characteristics:

• it is compatible with the Treaty, and thus easy to implement;
• it corrects an obvious mistake in the way the GSP was written; and
• it would help in the current slowdown.

With EU enlargement, the ECB faces a serious 'numbers' problem. Looking for a solution that is acceptable to all member states risks undermining the long-run credibility of the new institution.

References

Alesina, Alberto, Olivier Blanchard, Jordi Galí, Francesco Giavazzi and Harald Uhlig (2001a), 'Monitoring the ECB No. 3: defining a macro-economic framework for the euro area' (March), London: Centre for Economic Policy Research.

Alesina, Alberto, Olivier Blanchard, Jordi Galí, Francesco Giavazzi and Harald Uhlig (2001b), 'MECB No. 3: update' (July), London: Centre for Economic Policy Research.

Baldwin, Richard E., Erik Berglöf, Francesco Giavazzi and Mika Widgrén (2001), 'Twelve is company, twenty-seven is a crowd: preparing the ECB for enlargement' (September), CEPR Policy Paper, London: Centre for Economic Policy Research.

Blanchard, Olivier and F. Giavazzi (2002a), 'Current account deficits in the Euro area: the end of the Feldstein–Horioka puzzle?', *Brookings Papers on Economic Activity*, No. 2, Washington, DC: Brookings Institution.

(2002b), 'Reforms that can be done: improving the SGP through a proper accounting of public investment' (mimeo), Bocconi University and MIT.

Buiter, Willem (1981), 'Time preference and international lending and borrowing in an overlapping-generation model', *Journal of Political Economy*, 89 (4): 769–797.

De Gregorio, Jose and Holger Wolff (1994), 'Terms of trade, productivity, and the real exchange rate', NBER Working Paper No. 4807, National Bureau of Economic Research, Cambridge, MA.

Diamond, Peter (1965), 'National debt in a neoclassical growth model', *American Economic Review*, 55 (5): 1126–1150.

Estrada, A. and J. David Lopez-Salido (2001), 'Measuring Spanish technological change using sectorial data' (mimeo), Banco de España, Madrid.

Musgrave, R. A. (1939), 'The nature of budgetary balance and the case for the capital budget', *American Economic Review*, 29: 260–271.

5 | *The integration of EU banking markets*

JORDI GUAL

Introduction

The goal of this chapter is to provide an assessment of the EU policies that pursue the creation of a single banking market.[1] The chapter evaluates the degree of integration of EU banking markets and the impact of the integration process on the conduct, the structure and the performance of the industry at the EU level, and discusses whether current policies are the most appropriate instruments for market integration.

After this introduction, the second section of the chapter summarizes the key features of EU policy and compares this policy with alternative methods of market opening. The analysis stresses that market opening in regulated markets such as banking faces a difficult trade-off between the respect for domestic preferences and the elimination of regulations that protect local competitors and are not justified on efficiency grounds.

The third section provides an overview of recent research, which has looked at different indicators of market integration in EU banking and analyses the data on cross-border establishments and national and EU-wide concentration as key indicators of progress in European integration. In this respect, the US banking industry provides an interesting benchmark which is used whenever comparable information is available.

The fourth section analyses the impact of integration policies on the conduct, the structure and the performance of the banking industry. The objective is to assess whether EU integration has contributed to increasing the efficiency of the EU banking industry through cost reductions and lower markups. The study of changes in the degree of rivalry focuses on the behaviour and the determinants of the pass-through from interbank rates to retail rates. These changes are

---

[1] Comments by Bruno Cassiman are gratefully acknowledged.

considered together with the data on the restructuring of the industry through mergers and acquisitions and the evolution of efficiency and profitability measures.

A final section provides an integrative assessment, summarizing the key results of the chapter and evaluating the extent to which the changes in the degree of integration and the performance of the industry imply that the EU single market policies have achieved their objectives.

The integration policy of the EU in banking

The EU has been implementing banking directives for many years, with the goal of achieving a single EU banking market. This programme is part of a broader mandate to create a single market for services. In banking, a single market means that any provider of banking services can establish itself (or acquire banks) across the Union, and that customers can bank with any credit institution legally established in the Union. These are the well-known free trade and freedom of establishment principles. In the case of banking, the second principle includes not only the setting-up of subsidiaries that receive no different treatment from domestic banks but also foreign branches that need not be locally incorporated.

The problem is, of course, that achieving the goals of free trade and cross-border investment in banking is especially complex due to the fact that the industry is heavily regulated.

For the purposes of analysing the integration process, I will distinguish three types of regulation (see White, 1996). The first includes prudential regulation, that is, all those restrictions on banks which are introduced with the objective of mitigating the market failures that arise in the banking business (for example, negative externalities that provoke bank runs, or asymmetric information problems that lead to excessive risk taking). These regulations include solvency and own funds requirements, limits on large exposures and rules regarding participation in non-financial firms or activities. Deposit guarantee schemes which attempt to thwart the appearance of bank runs are also included under this heading. In general, all these restrictions impose a (private) cost on banks, but in principle they are justified as interventions with the goal of correcting a situation of market failure.

The second type of regulation comprises restrictions imposed directly on the structure of the industry and the conduct of business.

The conventional list of these regulations is very long, including direct restrictions on entry, limits on the number of competitors or the number of branches and the geographical scope of banks, direct rate regulation and rules on lines of business that banks can undertake or specific financial products that they can market. The justification of these measures has not in general been directly linked to a concern for market failures. They have been, however, pervasive in many countries. It is true that very often these measures soften competition and increase the franchise value of the banks, thus limiting the incentives for banks to engage in excessive risk taking. However, the increase in market power is not necessarily the most efficient way to handle the moral hazard problem; in addition, the economic regulations that limit entry do not deal directly with an externality problem and may easily be the result of pressure exerted by incumbent firms on the regulator. Similarly, regulations that limit the scope of banking activities or the freedom to determine prices can certainly reduce the riskiness of credit institutions, but they are not necessarily the most appropriate instruments for this regulatory objective.

A third type of regulation concerns the information that is required from credit institutions regarding both the characteristics of banking products and services, and the soundness of their financial situation. This regulation attempts to reduce the serious informational asymmetries which arise in the banking relationship. A depositor has little knowledge of the quality of the banking assets that he holds indirectly, and this may inefficiently limit the expansion of banking activities unless some control is imposed on the information provided by banks.

Regulatory restrictions lead to two sorts of problems that may undermine or call into question the integration process. First, some banking services may be subject to different regulatory treatment across the member states. For example, checking accounts (also called current accounts, especially in the UK) may or may not be allowed to provide interest. This difference in regulations could prevent the deployment of EU-wide product strategies and limit some of the scale advantages that the single market could provide. Second, credit institutions may be subject to a different set of regulatory restrictions. In certain countries, for example, banks may undertake insurance and investment banking activities while in other markets this is forbidden. This conflict was present, for example, in the trade agreements between Canada and the United States before the derogation of the Glass–Steagall Act. The act did not allow US credit institutions to undertake activities similar to those permitted to Canadian banks. In both cases, the conflicting regulatory situations lead to instances of asymmetric regulatory treatment across the Union that may distort business decisions in terms of both cross-border trade and establishment.

As a result of the complex layers of regulation that affect the industry, the integration process implies not only that barriers to trade and investment are eliminated, but also that some decisions have to be taken with regard to how a service consumed abroad is regulated, and how a firm is regulated when it operates abroad. At least three solutions are possible.

The first consists of the full harmonization of regulatory restrictions. Such a solution eliminates, of course, the problems of regulatory asymmetry, and it certainly paves the way for a fully integrated banking market. However, it is a solution which is very soon discarded as unfeasible in the absence of full political integration. This is because the regulation of financial products is very much linked to commercial and contract law, and this is an area where traditions differ substantially across countries.

A second alternative is the use of the national treatment principle (see, for example, Van Empel and Mörner, 2000). This principle states that foreign providers have to be allowed access to the local market and must be treated in all respects no differently from domestic providers. This principle allows each country to maintain different regulations, provided that there is no discrimination among providers on the grounds of country of origin. The national treatment principle is one of the cornerstones of the trade liberalization agreements for goods (GATT), but was not adopted as a basic principle in the trade agreement which covers financial services (GATS). In this agreement, granting national treatment as well as providing access is subject to negotiations. Countries joining the agreement commit only to the most-favoured-nation principle – and even then with some exemptions – and to the principles of transparency and the availability of national remedies.[2]

---

[2] The most-favoured-nation principle implies that any trade advantage that is conferred on one specific trade partner has to be extended to the rest. Measures dealing with prudential goals are not affected by the trade agreements.

The national treatment principle is straightforward with regard to foreign establishments, since it implies that foreign providers are subject to the local rules. It is, however, more controversial when referring to cross-border trade, as exemplified by the provisions in the North American Free Trade Agreement (NAFTA). This agreement goes beyond the terms of the GATS and incorporates explicitly the national treatment principle (Art. 1405). It applies both to subsidiaries (establishments) and cross-border providers. However, the agreement allows any of the parties to require the registration of cross-border financial service providers of another party, and of financial instruments (Art. 1404.3), and does not oblige any of the parties to allow cross-border selling of those services (the obligation of access under the national treatment principle 'does not require a Party to permit such providers to do business or solicit in its territory . . . each Party may define "doing business" and "solicitation" for purposes of this obligation').

Overall, the national treatment principle allows market access (establishment) and a substantial degree of free trade, but it is clearly insufficient if the objective is the creation of a single market. It leads to the maintenance of several regulatory regimes with which the credit institution has to comply if it wants to operate across the whole free trade area and, as shown in the case of NAFTA, it is difficult to apply in the case of cross-border services.

The third integration method is based on the mutual recognition principle. Mutual recognition implies that each country acknowledges the regulation of its partners and accepts service provision by foreign institutions as if they were domestic entities. Mutual recognition allows the maintenance of different rules in the participating countries, but the granting of market access without establishing a harmonized regulation implies that institutions from different countries will compete subject to different regulatory constraints. Since these constraints will usually undermine the competitive position of banks, regulatory institutions are likely to engage in a process of competitive deregulation, attempting to ensure that the entities under their regulatory control are not handicapped relative to their competitors. Moreover, banks are likely to alter their strategies – including their location – to take advantage of the more favourable regulatory environment. It appears, therefore, that mutual recognition could foster a high degree of market integration, but also undermine the effectiveness of regulations and lead to what sometimes is described as regulatory meltdown.

When attempting to integrate regulated industries such as banking, which of the three systems that we have reviewed is most appropriate? One way to answer this question is to assess the implications of each system for the three types of regulation distinguished above. Does the chosen integration method provide sufficient guarantees that sound regulatory tools remain in place?

The full harmonization process guarantees market integration and may also ensure compliance with prudential regulatory goals if the right instruments are put in place. Similarly, it can provide for the elimination of harmful economic regulation. However, to the extent that the harmonization affects information and consumer protection regulation, it can lead to a loss of diversity which should be taken into account as a negative impact.

The national treatment method provides a limited degree of integration but guarantees that national regulatory goals are maintained, for both prudential and information regulation. Economic regulation may be undermined by the integration process, since allowing market access on a non-discriminatory basis implies that domestic firms may face, in the domestic marketplace, foreign competitors which are regulated differently (and to their advantage) in their home country. Since economic regulation is not seriously grounded on any well-defined market failure problem, deregulation triggered by market access may be indeed a welcome process which erodes harmful market interventions.

Mutual recognition, finally, results also in a high degree of integration, but will lead to the disappearance of those regulations which either increase the cost of domestic institutions or divert banking activities abroad. This includes prudential rules fundamentally, and to a lesser degree information regulation and economic regulation. The process of market integration in the European Union has been based on the method of mutual recognition, although with some adjustments that attempt to limit the process of regulatory competition. Mutual recognition has been complemented by the establishment of harmonized standards with regard to prudential regulations. This is appropriate. It is clear that these regulations are targeting a well-defined and sound social objective. Since they impose costs on banks, reducing their international competitiveness, they could easily lead to regulatory arbitrage. Note also that the harmonizing regulation established a minimum standard and did not prevent individual countries from enforcing even stricter prudential requirements.

The EU integration process does not set any minimum standards with regard to economic regulation; in fact, it establishes the predominance of the universal banking model, allowing credit institutions to engage in both commercial and investment banking activities. Nor does it impose regulations on the provision of other financial services (such as insurance) or on other aspects of banking conduct. This approach is based on the belief that mixed competition will foster the lifting of economic regulations that are not justified by the existence of market failure (eliminating controls on rates, allowing the expansion of banking firms geographically and across financial activities etc.), on the understanding that the minimum prudential standards will ensure that this deregulation process does not lead to excessive risk taking and solvency problems.

As for the risk of excessive regulatory competition in the area of information regulation, the European Union has tackled the problem by introducing an exception to the mutual recognition principle. It allows the host country to regulate in this area. This amounts to using the national treatment rule for regulations that attempt to protect the consumer. In practice, this exception has been implemented through the introduction of the general good clause. This clause allows the domestic authorities to deny access to the domestic market to foreign providers or foreign financial services when it is deemed that the general interest is at risk.

Overall, the process of mutual recognition coupled with the harmonization of prudential regulation and the rules on host country control for consumer protection issues have allowed the process of EU banking integration to proceed much faster than in the past – when full harmonization was attempted – and achieve a deeper integration than can be obtained through the use of the national treatment principle (as in the NAFTA process).

Despite this progress, several issues remain highly controversial and, according to some observers, stand in the way of full integration. First, the competitive deregulation process has not led to similar degrees of liberalization across countries, with the persistence of some asymmetric regulation situations. For example, some peculiarities persist in terms of institutions in countries such as Germany, Spain, France and Greece. A second set of problems arises from the use of the general good clause as a tool to maintain regulatory control by the host country. For example, countries such as France do not allow interest-bearing checking

accounts and claim that allowing foreign banks to supply this product
would harm the general interest because it would trigger an increase
in the commissions paid by the less well-off customers.[3]

More generally, despite mutual recognition, the host country is still
allowed, in the name of the general good, to control key aspects of
the marketing and information provided for financial products (for
example, on UCITS)[4] and these regulations are perceived by foreign
banks as important restrictions that prevent the exploitation of scale
economies for the whole EU.

Finally, a third group of problems refers to the different national
regulation of certain products, particularly with regard to their tax
treatment. This excludes the straightforward case of tax discrimination
between providers of different origin (see Heinemann and Jopp, 2002:
52–53), which is clearly against EU law. Rather, it refers to the fact that
across the EU a similar product, such as a pension fund, must satisfy
very different sets of requirements to qualify for special tax treatment.[5]

As we have seen, the system of market integration adopted by the
EU is a combination of three alternative methods: mutual recognition
(with home country regulations), a limited dose of harmonization and
national treatment through the exceptions granted by the general good
clause that gives the host country control over certain issues. The con-
ceptual framework developed in this section allows us to analyse the
remaining contentious issues in a systematic way.

With regard to the asymmetric (and potentially distorting) regulatory
treatment of some institutions in certain countries, one way to tackle
the issue is through the use of the authority of the EU in terms of general
competition law. After all, this differential regulatory treatment will be
a matter of concern only if the different treatment of institutions has an
impact on competition, whether against domestic or foreign players.

[3] See Sun and Pelkmans, 1995. A recent case on the same issue has involved
a subsidiary of a Spanish saving bank.
[4] Undertakings for Collective Investments in Transferable Securities. See
Heinemann and Jopp, 2002: 52.
[5] The report to the European Roundtable for Financial Services (Heinemann
and Jopp, 2002) refers to the Riester products in Germany, which must
satisfy stringent conditions to qualify for tax advantages. Similar restraints
are imposed in other countries for the contributions to these funds to be
tax-deductible.

On the question of the use of the general good clause, the analysis is more complex. Consider a country A, which does not allow interest-bearing checking accounts, and a country B, which does. The general good clause may be used to prevent a firm from B offering its service in A directly through a branch or subsidiary (although no one can prevent a customer from A from banking in B and opening an interest-bearing checking account there). Similarly, consider another country A which does not allow early loan repayments and another country B that does. Can we use the general good principle to prevent a bank from B from operating in A directly (through branches or subsidiaries)?

In both cases, A is the more heavily regulated country and B is the less regulated one, and the introduction of the general good clause stops the competitive deregulation process. Both cases arise because harmonization has taken place at the level of definition of the banking licence but not at the level of individual products. Is the exception to mutual recognition justified in these instances? Is it justified, for example, in the case of checking accounts in terms of local preferences, say, for solvency, or to avoid transaction charges, if it is felt that this would hurt poor customers? To what extent can one argue that this is just a protectionist excuse?

As for leaving to host authorities the control of marketing, this may make sense if we are to respect national preferences, even if it implies a certain loss in terms of scale economies. Ultimately, two issues should be studied in detail. The first is the extent to which these local rules may in practice act as barriers to foreign providers. Second is the need for these local rules to assess whether home country rules exist that offer similar protection to the one that the domestic (host) regulators are trying to introduce.

Finally, when national regulations differ due to different tax treatments of financial products (and other social features), this makes sense to the extent that there is no harmonization of tax and social policy in the EU. Again, there might be some loss in terms of unfulfilled integration, but this may be counterbalanced by the respect of domestic preferences.

Are EU banking markets integrated?

The banking industry comprises a variety of market segments, in which the nature of competition is diverse and in which we would expect to observe different degrees of market integration. For each market segment, we can assess the extent of integration as it is usually done in trade theory. We can focus on the evolution of price convergence, or we can look at a quantity indicator, such as cross-border flows or, in the case of direct investment, the market share of foreign entities.

Price convergence implies that price differentials for the same financial service should be eliminated over time, or at least greatly reduced, down to the level justified by the existence of significant arbitrage or transportation costs.

As for quantities, it should be stressed that this is a complementary indicator. Indeed, the absence of cross-border flows (or the small market share of foreign competitors) need not be incompatible with a substantial degree of integration, provided that the threat of foreign entry/competition keeps the markets integrated – with price differences which do not exceed the costs of arbitrage.

In financial services, there is of course an additional channel of integration. The final customers (typically, companies on the borrowing side, families on the lending side) may access foreign markets indirectly to the extent that the financial intermediaries themselves become internationalized. For example, domestic investors may buy UCITS from local credit institutions that invest in foreign equities. Similarly, companies may issue bonds which are placed in the international market by a local institution.

Let us consider next the degree to which geographic market integration has been achieved in the EU for each market segment. The most integrated markets are the money and the government bond markets. These are markets in which the products are highly standardized and integration was practically achieved with the advent of the single currency, which eliminated the remaining segmentation of the markets due to currency denomination.

Consider, first, the interbank market. Table 5.1 shows how the spread between the German interest rate and the local rate has collapsed to zero for euro zone countries. It has also gone down significantly for the rest of the EU. It is worth pointing out that this practically full convergence has been achieved with an intra-EU market share of interbank claims of around 17 per cent, as reported by Danthine, Giavazzi and von Thadden for the end of 1999 (2000: table 4.2, p. 53). This confirms that these markets can become integrated even if the market shares of local players are fairly large. Adam *et al.* (2002) also demonstrate for

Table 5.1 *Average spreads before and after European monetary union*

	Interbank 3-month rates		Benchmark 10-year yields		Mortgage rates		Corporate loans rates	
	Before '99	After '99	Before '99	After '99	Before '99	After '99	Before '99	After '99
Austria	10	0	15	25	47	0.1	−89	−199
Belgium	7	0	32	31	−8	35	−332	−343
Denmark	80	53	85	37	n.a.	n.a.	−167	−246
Finland	40	0	84	22	19	−41	−249	−351
France	74	0	21	13	183	73	−142	−308
Greece	1059	380	n.a.	n.a.	n.a.	188	1234	413
Ireland	216	0	85	14	87	−49	202	87
Italy	404	0	262	32	488	43	251	−207
Luxembourg	n.a.	n.a.	−12	19	n.a.	n.a.	n.a.	n.a.
Netherlands	−12	0	−0.6	14	13	161	−435	−376
Portugal	316	0	204	33	376	−3	245	−248
Spain	299	0	208	28	213	−28	−54	−335
Sweden	224	−7	171	27	186	93	−45	−304
UK	308	180	130	19	166	141	n.a.	n.a.

Notes: Basis points. Spreads relative to German rates. The data before 1999 refer to the period January 1995–December 1998. The period after 1999 refers to January 1999–September 2001.

N.a.: not available.

Source: Adam *et al.*, 2002.

this market that beta convergence (the reduction in the dispersion of rates) has accelerated in recent times and that, in fact, full convergence was achieved thanks to European monetary union (EMU).

As for the public bond market, the same sorts of data show that the spreads have gone down dramatically. They do not collapse to zero as in the interbank market, but there are reasons to believe they have been reduced to a level compatible with an integrated market, as they are similar to the spreads within the United States (see Danthine, Giavazzi and von Thadden, 2000: figure 4.3). The remaining positive spreads correspond to credit and liquidity risks, which need not go away with market integration, although Danthine, Giavazzi and von Thadden (2000) argue that the market may end up eliminating even the liquidity risk associated with some issuers. In the public bond market, convergence has been as fast as in the interbank market, even though there remains a degree of dispersion in rates which has not disappeared with EMU.

With regard to the private bond market, this has been historically fairly internationalized from the point of view of the firms present in the marketplace. The process of financial integration, and in particular the adoption of a single currency, has contributed very significantly to its further expansion[6] and, most importantly for our purposes, it has increased the degree of integration from the point of view of the location of investors. Already in 2000, Danthine, Giavazzi and von Thadden (2000) reported that an increasing proportion of euro issues from large firms in specific member states were being placed in other EU markets. More systematically, recent research by Adam *et al.* (2002) has looked at the extent to which bond market funds in the EU have gradually moved to Europe-wide investment strategies. These authors conclude that the adoption of the euro led to a large increase in the asset share of internationally investing bond funds in eurozone countries, a process that has not taken place in the EU states that have not adopted the single currency.

Adam *et al.* (2002) consider similar measures with regard to stock exchanges. Consolidation in this market is proving difficult, but integration is taking place indirectly to the extent that investment institutions – and in many countries this means the leading universal banks – manage their investment funds, and UCITS in general, from

[6] See, for example, European Commission 2001: 142.

an EU-wide perspective. Adam *et al.* analyse the changes in the asset composition of investment institutions across the EU. They conclude that, with the exception of France, Spain and Greece, the percentage of equity funds marketed in EU member states that have an EU-wide investment strategy increased significantly between 1997 and 2001.[7]

Consider next the commercial banking market. I will focus on corporate loans for business and mortgages for residential customers. These are the markets for which comparable interest rates across the EU were collected by Adam *et al.* (2002). These rates show that price differences have not diminished over the years and in particular since EMU (see table 5.1). The analysis of Adam *et al.* also shows little beta convergence over time (2002: tables 5.1–5.3). This evidence is consistent with the fact there has not been an upward trend in the presence of foreign credit institutions in individual EU retail banking markets (see Buch and Heinrich, 2002; ECB, 1999b). The reduced penetration of foreign banks in domestic markets is not necessarily in contradiction with other trends, which show that EU banks have become more internationalized over time. The data reported by the Bank for International Settlements (BIS) show that the share of foreign assets in total assets of EU-based banks has been growing continuously over the past ten years.[8] As argued before, this internationalization takes place through the lending and funding activities of domestic banks.

For the purpose of examining the degree of integration of EU banking markets, these internationalization trends deserve closer examination. In particular, it is interesting to examine the relative position of non-EU and EU banks in this process, and whether the process of integration is taking place through branches or through subsidiaries. Tables 5.2 and 5.3 provide a summary of the relevant data for the period 1999–2001.

---

[7] The integration process could also have taken place for the three countries above if, instead of using domestic funds, they had increased their share of foreign assets by acquiring foreign investment funds directly. This information is, however, unavailable. The results for these three countries could also be due to divergences in the way funds are classified.

[8] Between 1990 and 1995, the international assets (classified by nationality of ownership, table 8 of the BIS International Banking Statistics; see *BIS Quarterly Review*) of EU15 banks that report to the BIS grew by 10.6 per cent per year, and the rate was 12.7 per cent between 1996 and 2001. Total assets for the same group of countries grew between 1997 and 2000 at an average rate of 6.9 per cent (data from ECB, 2002b, table 8).

Table 5.2 *Number of foreign branches and subsidiaries in the EU banking market*

Intra-EEA				Non-EEA			
Branches	*1997*	*2001*	*% change*	*Branches*	*1997*	*2001*	*% change*
EU	420	497	18	EU	297	216	−27
EU except UK and Luxembourg	259	356	37	EU except UK and Luxembourg	138	95	−31
UK and Luxembourg	161	141	−12	UK and Luxembourg	159	121	−24

Intra-EEA				Non-EEA			
Subsidiaries	*1997*	*2001*	*% change*	*Subsidiaries*	*1997*	*2001*	*% change*
EU	301	328	9	EU	252	212	−16
EU except UK and Luxembourg	183	222	21	EU except UK and Luxembourg	128	100	−22
UK and Luxembourg	118	106	−10	UK and Luxembourg	124	112	−10

Note: Sample of ten countries in the EU (excluded countries are Austria, Denmark, Greece, Ireland and Sweden).
Source: Own elaboration from ECB, 2002b.

An examination of the trends in terms of number of both units (table 5.2) and volume of assets (table 5.3) reveals two significant facts. The first is that there is a clear trend towards dominance of branches over subsidiaries (particularly in terms of units, less so in assets), although, as pointed out by Dermine (2002), the latter form remains important and that may be an indication of insufficient integration given the trends observed in the United States. Rosengreen (2002) uses the US benchmark and concludes that the persistence of subsidiaries may indeed reflect incomplete integration. He stresses, however, that the choice of incorporating in different jurisdictions is often related to tax and legal advantages offered by the host state. Such differences are, of course, more likely in the EU.

The second fact is that the trend towards a reduced presence of non-EEA[9] banks continued strongly in the period 1997–2001, confirming

[9] The European Economic Area includes the European Union plus Iceland, Liechtenstein and Norway. The Agreement creating the EEA was negotiated between the Union and seven member countries of the EFTA and signed in May 1992. Subsequently one of these (Switzerland) decided, after a referendum, not to participate and three others joined the Union. The EEA Agreement entered into force on 1 January 1994. The EEA has been maintained because member countries which are not EU member countries wished to participate in the single market without the full responsibilities of EU membership.

Table 5.3 Assets of foreign branches and subsidiaries in the EU banking market

Intra-EEA

Branches	1997	2001	% change 97–00	% change 97–01
EU	1261184	1941947	44	54
EU except UK and Lux.	316303	447523	37	41
UK and Lux.	944881	1494424	46	58

Subsidiaries	1997	2000	% change 97–00
EU	802898	1189829	48
EU except UK and Lux.	412486	681378	65
UK and Lux.	390412	508451	30

Non-EEA

Branches	1997	2001	% change 97–99	% change 97–01
EU	1076806	1314853	–6	22
EU except UK and Lux.	179618	98740	–41	–45
UK and Lux.	897188	1216113	1	36

Subsidiaries	1997	1999	% change 97–99
EU	485899	472122	–3
EU except UK and Lux.	241810	208307	–14
UK and Lux.	244089	263815	8

Note: Sample of ten countries in the EU (excluded countries are Austria, Denmark, Greece, Ireland and Sweden). All asset figures in millions of euros.

Source: Own elaboration from ECB, 2002b.

Table 5.4 *Number of banking mergers and acquisitions in the EU*

	Geographical breakdown					
	1995	1996	1997	1998	1999	2000 (up to June)
TOTAL	326	343	319	434	497	234
Domestic	275	293	270	383	414	172
Intra-EU	20	7	12	18	27	23
Extra-EU	31	43	37	33	56	39
	Breakdown by size of domestic transactions					
	1995	1996	1997	1998	1999	2000
% large	18%	10%	13%	13%	12%	22%
% small	82%	90%	87%	87%	88%	78%

Source: ECB 2000a.
Large: Mergers and acquisitions involving at least one firm with assets of one billion euros or more.

the tendency already present in the data covering the early 1990s and reported in an ECB report in the late 1990s (1999b).

An additional indicator of integration that is sometimes used is the geographical breakdown of mergers and acquisitions. This indicator suffers from the same drawbacks as the foreign market share and, in fact, if cross-border consolidation advanced, it would be also captured by the market share data. This information can, however, be particularly instructive when we compare EU trends with those of the United States. Table 5.4 shows very clearly that the consolidation that took place during the second half of the 1990s was characterized (as in earlier periods: see Gual and Neven, 1993) by its domestic nature. This is in sharp contrast to what has been observed in the United States, where, as summarized by DeYoung (1999), most of the mergers and acquisitions have taken place between banks from different regions. In the United States, moreover, antitrust activity may be restricting local consolidation, while in Europe very few domestic mergers have been blocked by regulators.

An alternative and complementary way to look at this is to analyse the evolution of the national concentration figures and the EU concentration ratio and compare this with the US outcome as reported by DeYoung (1999). If mergers are taking place within borders, national concentration increases while EU-wide concentration need not increase. This is what has happened in Europe (see figures 5.1 and 5.2), but not in the United States, where local concentration indices have been comparatively constant, while the federal concentration ratio has increased markedly.

The divergence of trends in concentration in the United States and the EU can be complemented by an analysis of concentration trends at the world level. Although it is difficult to collect the appropriate data, the information generated by the BIS project on consolidation provides a close enough approximation (see table 5.5). These data seem to indicate that, indeed, the global process of internationalization and opening of banking markets is leading to a trend of increased concentration, whether we look at the top twenty or the top forty world banks.[10] If that is the case, it is clear that we should observe even faster trends of increased concentration in areas that, thanks to deregulation and market-opening measures, are becoming single markets, such as the EU and the United States. As hypothesized elsewhere (Gual, 1999), such a process of consolidation would not accompany market enlargement if competition in the banking sector were based on conventional variables (with scale economies that may be significant, but of an exogenous nature, related to the technical aspects of the production process). Conversely, if we observe that market enlargement stimulates increased concentration, this may be due to the fact that the banking industry is increasingly characterized by competition in sunk fixed costs such as reputation, brand or the advantages of size related to the 'too big to fail' perception by customers. If banking is characterized by these 'endogenous sunk costs', then the aggregate EU figures in figures 5.1 and 5.2 look all the more surprising. The slow increase in EU-wide concentration would thus confirm that political factors prevent cross-border consolidation.

Before finalizing the analysis of integration, it is worth recalling a very direct piece of evidence that has been highlighted repeatedly by the European Commission and that underlines the extent to which the single market project remains unfulfilled. The cost of cross-border retail payments compared to domestic transactions continues to be

---

[10] The data refer to the banks of thirteen leading countries.

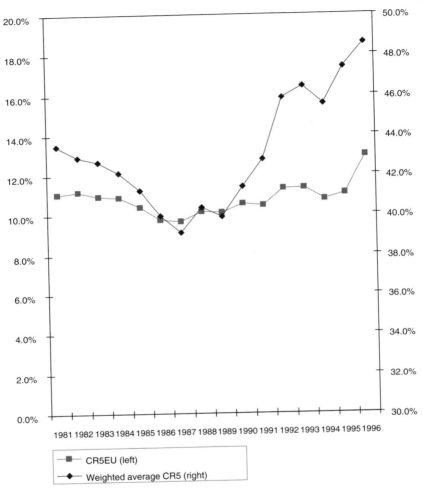

Source: Updated from Gual, 1999, based on data from *The Banker* and the OECD bank profitability dataset.
Weights: Total assets of each national banking system.
CR5EU: The five-firm concentration ratio for the overall EU market (the percentage of total banking assets corresponding to the top five banks).
Weighted average CR5: The weighted average of the five-firm concentration ratios of each of the EU member states.

Figure 5.1 National and EU-wide banking concentration 1981–1996

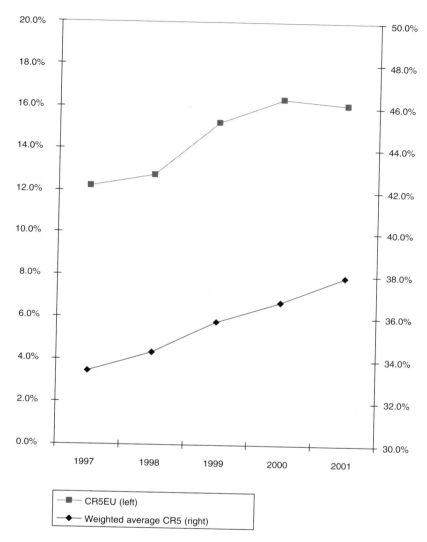

Source: Weighted concentration data computed using data from ECB, 2002b. EU-wide
concentration computed using *The Banker* for the assets of the five largest EU banks.
Note: See figure 5.1 for definitions.

Figure 5.2 National and EU-wide banking concentration 1997–2001

Table 5.5 *Worldwide banking concentration*

| | Assets of largest banks as a percentage of total banking assets | |
	1990	1997
Top 20	22%	25%
Top 30	28%	34%
Top 40	33%	41%
Top 50	37%	46%

Source: Own elaboration on the basis of Group of Ten, 2001. The following thirteen banking systems are included: Australia, Belgium, Canada, France, Germany, Italy, Japan, Netherlands, Spain, Sweden Switzerland, United Kingdom and USA.

high and has not fallen significantly over the last ten years.[11] In 1993, the average charge for an EU cross-border credit transfer of € 100 was € 23.93. Eight years later, the charge had risen to € 24.09, reflecting the high degree of segmentation of EU markets in this area.[12]

To conclude, the analysis of the integration process undertaken in this section points to the following key results. First, integration has taken place, albeit at different paces depending on the market segment. This is fully consistent with what we would expect given the differences in the nature of competition in the existing lines of business of the industry. A second important result is that branches play an increasing role as a way to penetrate foreign markets, although – as discussed by Dermine (2002) – it may be a bit surprising that subsidiaries are still so important, and this questions the effectiveness of EU integration measures. Finally, the data from 1997–2001 confirm the previous trend of a declining presence of non-EU banks, suggesting that the successful integration of EU banking markets may be generating a 'trade diversion' effect.[13] That is, lower barriers within the EU lead to increased

[11] As reported by the EU Economic and Financial Committee. See European Commission, 2002.
[12] This is also pointed out by the ECB, 2002a.
[13] The ECB has recently provided an analysis of the retreat of Japanese and US banks. See ECB, 2002b.

competitiveness of EU institutions relative to their non-EU rivals, despite the fact that non-EU banks benefit also from an enlarged local EU market.

Conduct, structure and performance in EU banking markets

The ultimate goal of the European Union integration policy in banking is not simply the creation of a large internal market. Rather, this policy goal is put forward as a key building block towards the final objective of achieving a more efficient EU financial services market which ultimately will contribute to higher economic growth and employment across the Union.[14]

In principle, a large single market will contribute to the development of deeper and more efficient financial services through well-known mechanisms. The larger market should in theory lead to a more competitive environment, with the development of stronger credit institutions, able to offer a wider and more complex array of financial products and services. Several reports commissioned by the EU have stressed the relationship between market size and efficiency and have attempted to estimate the magnitude of these effects (Economic Research Europe, 1996). More recently, the same types of argument have been brought forward with regard to integration in financial services other than commercial banking (Heinemann and Jopp, 2002; London Economics, 2002).

It is therefore necessary to assess the extent to which the increased integration of EU markets, confirmed in the previous section, is having its predicted beneficial effects on the structure and performance of EU banking. Let us start by looking at the degree of competition and move on to changes in market structure.[15]

Has integration in fact led to increased rivalry, as was predicted? Measuring the degree of rivalry is notoriously difficult, as has been

---

[14] On the relation between the efficiency of the financial services industry and economic growth, see Giannetti *et al.*, 2002, European Commission, 2001 and the study by Heinemann and Jopp, 2002. See also Demirgüç-Kunt and Levine, 2001.

[15] For reasons of space, I do not deal with issues of structure that affect the activities of banks in areas such as securities and insurance. Nor do I discuss in detail the presence of commercial banks in the UCITS market and in the disintermediation process (see for example Dermine, 2002).

stressed by a long tradition of research in the field of industrial organization. In recent years there has been a growing literature (the new empirical industrial organization literature launched by Tim Bresnahan and others)[16] that has emphasized the need to estimate structural models of oligopoly competition. This approach has been sparsely applied to banking (see, for example, the paper by Neven and Röller, 1999), and certainly not with the goal of directly testing the extent to which the wider integration of EU banking markets has spurred wider rivalry.

Nevertheless, the characteristics of competition in retail banking markets provide an easy-to-implement test of rivalry which is not a direct measurement of the degree of competition but very often a sufficiently close approximation. This is the so-called pass-through test, which is based on the idea of assessing the degree of rivalry as captured by the extent to which changes in money market rates are passed through to retail rates.

This method makes sense if we can decouple the loan and deposit markets and assume that the money market rate provides an appropriate measure of the relevant opportunity costs for banks, both in terms of funding and in terms of allocating their investable funds. If that is the case, one can argue that the cost of funds in the money market is a good approximation to the short-run marginal costs, which should form the basis of pricing. It is then easy to construct a model (known very often in the literature as the Klein–Monti model) in which retail rates (whether loan or deposit) depend – in the oligopolistic equilibrium – on money market rates. For a representative bank in the market, indexed by j, the first-order equilibrium condition which reflects profit maximization in the relevant market[17] looks as follows:

$$\frac{r_{jt} - i_t}{r_{jt}} = \frac{1}{e_{jt}} \qquad [1]$$

where i_t is the interbank rate, r_{jt} is the retail rate (deposit or loans) and e is the elasticity of the demand for loans (or supply of deposits) function faced by the bank. Equation [1] is of course a standard relation capturing the equilibrium between (short-run) marginal costs and perceived

---

[16] See, for example, Bresnahan, 1989, and more recently for differentiated product markets Nevo, 2000.

[17] The basic equations are sketched here for the loan market, but a similar framework applies to deposits.

marginal revenue. With the introduction of additional restrictions, and aggregating over banks for each retail market, expression [1] can be transformed into [2] for the purposes of econometric analysis:

$$r_t = \mu i_t,$$ [2]

where μ is a function of the elasticities faced by each firm, the degree of co-ordination between banks and the number of firms (for details, see Gual, 1993). In the simplest case, that of a monopoly, the relation between μ and the elasticity of demand e is given by:

$$\mu = \frac{1}{1 + \frac{1}{e}}.$$ [3]

The parameter μ provides a good proxy of the degree of rivalry. Equation [2] is fairly intuitive: in more competitive markets the elasticity of demand is high (e is large in absolute value) and a change in the market interest rate will translate to a large degree into changes in the retail rate (μ is close to one). In general, the elasticity, which determines the degree of market power, will depend on the existence of substitutes[18] as well as on the degree of co-ordination or collusion between existing market players.

The relevance of this simple relationship has to be qualified. There might be several sources of rigidities which need not reflect lack of competition, for example, if the interest rates being compared correspond to aggregates of financial services with different maturities, or if menu costs are a significant source of price rigidity. More importantly, rates may be rigid due to the existence of asymmetric information. For example, when interbank rates go up, banks may not translate all the price increase into higher retail rates, since they know that this is likely to lead to a worsening of the loan portfolio (see De Bondt, 2002: 9). Finally, rigidities may appear to the extent that banking competition is characterized by important switching costs (Klemperer, 1987). If banking clients face significant costs for switching banks, this may lead banks to compete on the basis of market share, anticipating the effect of current rate setting on the extent of market share and captive clients in the future. Such a dynamic competitive set-up implies that

---

[18] The response of retail rates may also depend on the level of interest rates if the demand or supply schedules are not isoelastic.

banks take into account not only current interbank rates in the process of setting retail rates, but also their expected behaviour in the future. This may lead to more sluggish movements of rates which need not be the result of non-competitive behaviour. It will also imply that, in terms of the specification of [2], current retail rates will depend not only on current interbank rates, but also on future rates, as anticipated by the yield curve (for an application of this, see Gual, 1993).

Despite these shortcomings, pass-through analysis provides a much better indicator of the extent of competition than the use of simple markups (whether absolute or in percentage terms), since the markups will be affected by both market power and cost differences. It is also better than the conventional intermediation margin (net interest income over assets) since this margin suffers from the same problem, as well as from differences in asset composition (see also ECB, 2000b).

During the 1990s, several researchers looked at a variety of specifications of the pass-through model. Two of the most recent papers have looked at the EU retail markets precisely over the period that witnessed the process of liberalization and integration.[19] Mojon (2000) provides an analysis of the magnitude of the pass-through effect and assesses whether it went down with the opening-up of the markets in the 1990s. Corvoisier and Gropp (2001) go beyond this assessment and consider whether the trend of increased concentration that we have observed in many EU countries has countervailed the forces that led to increased competition as a result of the process of EU integration.

Mojon (2000) finds that interest rate rigidity is pervasive and, in common with previous studies on the subject, more important in the short run than over the longer term. Similarly, his study shows that differences across products and countries are substantial. The study also confirms the asymmetry of the pass-through. In the case of loans, rate increases are more easily passed on to consumers than rate decreases, while the opposite is true for deposit rates. This result, observed also in the US market, is consistent with a competition model in which switching costs are important and in which banks may set today's rates taking into account how this alters their future market share. For example, for the deposit market when interest rates go up, the gains from increased

---

[19] Another recent piece of work by Schüler and Heinemann (2002) looks at these issues using cointegration techniques. They find little integration for the consumer loans market and the savings deposit market.

Table 5.6 *Evidence on the interest rate pass-through*

	1979–88	1988–98
All	0.50	0.45
Credit	0.59	0.59
Breakdown by borrower		
Short-term credit to firms	0.83	0.78
Mortgages	0.34	0.31
Breakdown by country		
Belgium	0.31	0.56
France	0.79	0.75
Germany	0.74	0.66
Italy	0.90	0.62
Netherlands	0.76	0.75
Spain	0.17	0.28
Deposits	0.33	0.20
Breakdown by country		
Germany	0.76	0.35
Italy	0.27	0.14
Netherlands	0.10	0.19
Spain	0.01	0.11

Source: Mojon, 2000, table 5.2b.

future market share are worth comparatively less (future profits from larger market share are more heavily discounted), and this will mean that banks may have an incentive to focus on profitability, by moderately raising their rates and increasing the markup. Conversely, if rates go down, the present value of future profits goes up and banks will be more interested in fully adjusting their rate downwards. Deposit rates will therefore be stickiest on their way up.

Mojon (2000) finds that deposit markets are stickier than credit markets on average. The most competitive markets appear to be those corresponding to short-term credit to firms. At the country level, Spain, Belgium and the Netherlands show the least flexibility (see table 5.6). Most interesting for our purposes is the analysis of how the level of the pass-through changes within the sample period, which comprises 1979–98. Mojon divides the sample in two periods, 1979–88 and 1988–98, and shows that stickiness goes down for several countries

and markets, as predicted if competition has increased. However, this
is certainly not the case for all instances.

Mojon goes on to analyse the determinants of the differences in the
pass-through across countries and time. The results are revealing. He
shows that a variable capturing the extent of deregulation through
the adoption of the single banking market directives is an important
contributor, in terms of explaining the magnitude of the pass-through
as well as its asymmetry.

Corvoisier and Gropp (2001) do not look directly at the pass-
through. Rather, starting from a Klein–Monti model of banking competition, they specify a regression model in which the loan markup is
a function of several structural variables, in particular, measures of the
degree of concentration in the market. They try to ascertain the extent
to which the magnitude of the markup can be explained by measures
of concentration. They find that, for loans and demand deposits, the
trend towards increased concentration has limited the reduction of the
markup. This is not the case, however, in the markets for savings and
time deposits.

One explanation of these results is that the markets for loans and
demand deposits have poorer substitutes. With the development of
UCITS and other investment vehicles, substitution away from deposits
which are not needed for transactions is easier. By contrast, loan financing can be substituted only by direct financing, and demand deposits
are used for transactions, with very few alternatives available.

That the trend towards increased competition has been softened by
the sharp increase in concentration seems to be confirmed by the fact
that in Europe most mergers have not been used as an attempt to
expand abroad (see pp. 135–147) but rather as a way to rationalize at
home and possibly preserve market power.

Indeed, the trends in national concentration data confirm that over
the period 1997–2001, concentration of local markets increased.[20] As
shown in figure 5.3, in the current phase the markets undergoing the
biggest changes in concentration are the biggest and least concentrated
markets.

We see, therefore, that the integration process has proceeded during the 1990s, with a limited effect on the degree of competition as

[20] For previous years, see ECB, 2000a, and Group of Ten, 2001. However,
the data are not fully coincident due to the use of different methodologies.

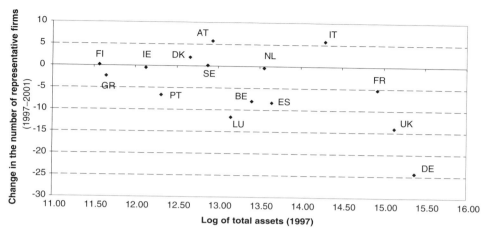

Source: Own elaboration from ECB, 2002b. The number of representative firms is the inverse of the Herfindahl index. It is the number of symmetric firms which would lead to the same level of concentration as registered by the actual Herfindahl index.

Figure 5.3 Market size and changes in banking concentration

captured by the changes in the markup, but with a substantial impact on the structure of the market, as measured both by changes in the concentration of the market through mergers and acquisitions, as well as by changes in the diversification of banks and their international exposures. Ultimately, however, it is important to assess whether the industry restructuring that has been triggered by the European integration has led to increased welfare for EU citizens through the creation of a more efficient EU banking industry, and whether these efficiency gains have been transmitted to consumers in the form of lower markups, or to shareholders through profits.

Assessing efficiency is fairly complex, however. It can be attempted by estimating cost functions and production efficiency frontiers, or rather by examining simple balance sheet measures which are common in the industry – such as the cost–income ratio or ratios such as operating expenses (or staff costs) relative to non-bank deposits. The Group of Ten (2001) and Dermine (2002) provide recent surveys of the analytical work, and the descriptive data (covering the period 1990–7) have been analysed by the ECB reports (1999a, 1999b) and are available from the OECD bank profitability dataset. The literature review by Dermine and the Group of Ten, as well as the analysis of the data in the latter reports, confirm (table 5.5 in Group of Ten (2001), comparing the United States, the EU and Japan) that cost–income ratios tend to be somewhat smaller for large banks, but not necessarily for banks above 50 billion dollars in assets,[21] and that, within each bank category by size, there appears to be a large divergence in terms of efficiency, suggesting, as advanced some time ago by Humphrey (1987), that factors other than scale economies play a much more important role as a source of cost differences across banks. The report by the Group of Ten concludes that mergers and acquisitions 'do not significantly improve cost . . . There is evidence in favour of exploiting scale economies in retail banking up to a certain size (well below that of the most recent very large deals)', and that 'Economies of scope are harder to pin down; there is no clear-cut evidence of their existence' (2001: 254–5).

As for balance sheet data in the EU, the trend observed for these efficiency ratios is of a very moderate reduction. The data cover one major business cycle, and the key ratios typically worsen during 1993 and 1994, improving later on and sometimes achieving by the late 1990s levels which are better than those of 1990. As reported by ECB (1999a, 1999b), it is clear that the industry has rationalized in terms of reducing the number of banks, branches or staff, say, per thousand inhabitants.[22] It is not obvious, however, that this rationalization has translated into greater economic efficiency.

Another way to assess whether the process of integration has allowed European banks to reap the benefits of increased scale is to analyse the extent to which consolidation has increased the average size of banks, and the extent to which there has been a convergence in average bank size across the EU. The latter would reflect that banks in small countries are increasingly scaling their activities not on the basis of the domestic market, but rather of the EU market. This analysis can be done using the whole size distribution of credit institutions, or with a summary measure such as the average size. Instead of the size of the simple average bank, figure 5.4 provides the size of the representative bank: a summary measure based on the Herfindahl concentration index (HHI)

---

[21] Average for the period 1994–7. See table 5.5 in Group of Ten, 2001. The category with the lowest cost–income ratio comprises banks between $20 and $50 billion in assets.

[22] The data for operating expenses as a percentage of non-bank assets is available in ECB, 1999a, tables A.10 and A.11. For the cost–income ratio, see ECB, 1999b, table 9.

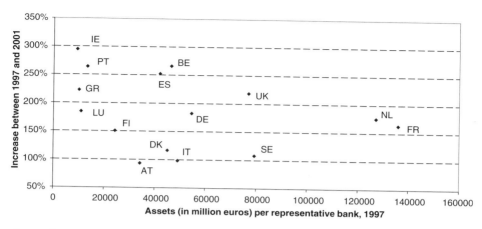

Source: Own elaboration from ECB, 2002b.

Figure 5.4 Size of the representative bank

which takes into account not only how many banks there are but also their relative market shares.[23]

The evolution of these indicators over the period 1997–2001 shows that consolidation and organic growth have only partially removed the striking differences in bank size across the Union, and that the size of banks continues to be small and relatively unchanged in several markets such as Finland, Austria, Denmark and Italy (see figure 5.4). These data support the idea that concentration processes based on national mergers have been a rather limited mechanism to enhance the efficiency of the industry.

Measurement problems become even more acute when we move on to assess profitability. A favoured industry standard is the analysis of ROE (return on equity). Using the same sources as before, the data seem to indicate that over the 1990s average industry profitability for the EU has been fairly stable at around 10 per cent, with only a moderate cyclical decline during the 1993 recession.[24]

---

[23] Instead of assets/number of banks, I compute assets/number of equivalent banks (NE), where NE=1/HHI. NE is the number of firms of equal market share which lead to an equivalent level of concentration (to the same HHI).

[24] See ECB, 1999b, table 9. Data on return on equity are for the period 1990–7. The Group of Ten report (2001) provides more recent harmonized data (based on the OECD bank profitability dataset) which do not change this overall view.

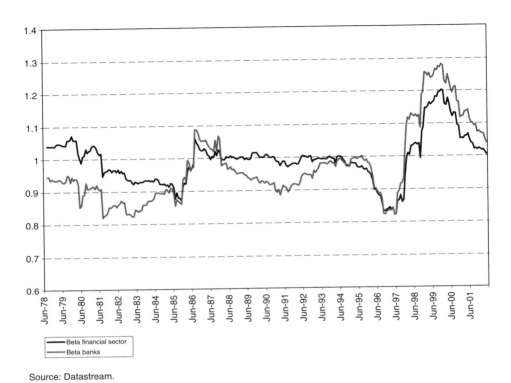

Source: Datastream.

Figure 5.5 The profitability of banking and financial intermediaries

The use of an accounting measure such as ROE is, of course, debatable on the usual grounds (see Schmalensee, 1989). Moreover, in the particular case of EU banking, an industry that has gone through such a remarkable period of turbulence with deregulation, ROE has special shortcomings. Indeed, given the nature of the banking business, the appropriate benchmark for profitability should take into account not only the return on invested funds, but also its variability, since this has a direct impact on the solvency of a credit institution. Indeed, deregulation and integration allow banks to engage in a variety of new activities and markets. New revenue can accrue from these new areas and compensate for reduced margins in conventional banking. However, it could well be the case that this maintained profitability is achieved at the cost of increased variance.

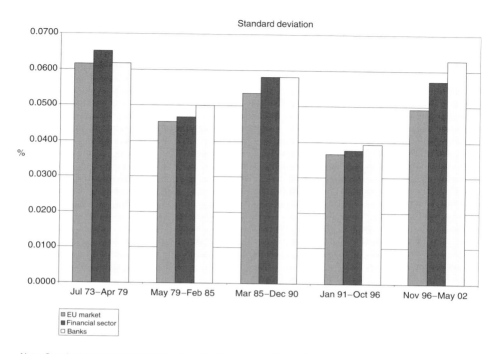

Note: Standard deviations of monthly returns for the corresponding periods.
Source: Own elaboration with data from Datastream.

Figure 5.6 The variability of returns in EU banking

In fact, this is approximately what the evidence suggests for the case of the aggregate EU banking industry. As shown in figures 5.5 and 5.6, it appears that the sector-specific market risk associated with banking activities has been increasing over recent years, especially compared to the larger industry aggregate that includes the entire financial sector. In a similar vein, figure 5.6 highlights the clear trend of the industry: a growing volatility of returns, higher than that of the financial sector or the market as a whole.

Overall, I conclude that integration has not led to a significant change in the degree of price competition in the industry (banks' rate-setting behaviour has not changed much). Rather, it has triggered dramatic changes in market structure, with consolidation in many national markets. It is not clear whether this process has improved the efficiency of the industry, but in any case it appears to have allowed industry participants to maintain their overall profitability. Nevertheless, the changing nature of banking, particularly in terms of revenue streams, with the increase in non-interest income as financial margins have deteriorated with the decline in interbank rates during the 1990s, implies that this maintenance of profitability has been coupled with a marked increase in the variability of banking returns.

Concluding remarks

Has EU policy been effective at integrating EU banking markets? This chapter has attempted to answer this question while stressing that market integration is not an end in itself, but rather that the final goal of the policy is to create a more efficient EU-wide banking market, while preserving such regulatory interventions as are firmly grounded in the market failures inherent in the banking industry.

As a consequence, any analysis of the effectiveness of the policy should be based on a broad assessment which takes into account not only the extent of integration of markets, but also how the market opening policies have impacted upon the performance of the industry from a private and social perspective.

The EU policy in this area has been based on the principle of mutual recognition. This method of integration implies that countries recognize each other's regulatory regime. It is a method of market opening for regulated industries which is more ambitious than the conventional trade approach based on the national treatment principle (market access with no discrimination of foreign companies), but less so than a full harmonization approach, in which all firms compete subject to the same regulatory framework.

Since mutual recognition can trigger a competitive deregulation process, the general principle was complemented with a minimum harmonization level for prudential regulations. Similarly, in the area of regulation of the information received by bank clients, the EU policy has also introduced exemptions, allowing the national treatment principle (host country control).

This eclectic integration method implies that the competitive deregulation process has basically impacted upon economic regulations that do not pursue well-defined efficiency goals. The method has therefore been quite successful at triggering the opening of markets and the demise of arbitrary regulatory constraints on the activities of financial intermediaries.

The degree of integration of banking markets has increased as a result of the EU single market policy and the adoption of the single currency. However, the integration is far from complete in retail markets, for several reasons.

First, in retail markets there are important natural and strategic barriers to entry which tend to keep markets segmented despite the introduction of market opening policies. Natural barriers such as language and distance imply that retail markets may continue to follow national borders (and even smaller geographical areas) for quite some time. Strategic barriers can also block market integration. Competition in retail banking is based on the deployment of assets such as branch network, brand and reputation (in part associated with bank size), and incumbent credit institutions may try to deploy these strategic assets in an attempt to gain competitive advantage in the process of market integration.

Indeed, an analysis of the conduct and the changes in the structure of the industry in recent years shows that the industry has reacted to the double pressure of integration and the single currency with an increase in the concentration of domestic markets, as a way to rationalize costs and protect market power. Such a competitive reaction is consistent with the observed evolution of competition, which has increased only mildly and for a few market segments (a limited effect in terms of the flexibility of the markup), and with the stability of overall profitability.

The strategic reaction of incumbent banks through domestic consolidation implies that some of the goals of integration have not been achieved. Markups could have declined faster, pricing could be more flexible and banks could have increased their size by way of cross-border mergers, in which the benefits of scale are clearer, according to most empirical studies. It appears that, in some instances, political constraints have prevented the cross-border consolidation process. Similarly, in certain member states, political interference may have allowed the achievement of very large concentration levels despite their potentially negative effect on bank clients.

Despite its limited impact on the degree of competition, the new competitive environment prompted by deregulation and integration has forced banks to diversify, increase their lines of business and engage in financial innovation, with an overall increase in business risk and the volatility of profits. These trends may have prudential implications, although it seems that those can be tackled with the harmonized solvency standards. It is uncertain, however, whether this process of increased volatility has impacted upon banks operating at the EU level, where potential solvency problems may have an impact extending beyond the country that controls the bank in terms of prudential regulations (see Dermine, 2002).

A second key reason why the integration process is not complete in retail banking has to do with the exceptions introduced in the integration process by allowing host country control in certain areas. These exceptions, which allow the imposition of local regulations when the general interest is at risk, should, in principle, ensure that domestic preferences are properly taken into account in the integration process. It is clear, however, that the preservation of the general good can be used as a legal instrument with protectionist objectives. The pre-eminence of local rules should be accepted only when it can be shown that no comparable home country regulation serves the same objective, and that the local rule cannot be used discriminatorily against foreign providers. Competition policy, a policy which can be forcefully deployed by EU authorities to preserve the general EU interest, should be used in these instances, if local regulators use the general interest argument as a protectionist device.

The process of assessing whether these exceptions to the mutual recognition principle are appropriate or not is bound, however, to be fairly complex and politically controversial. Integration will be limited, on the other hand, because other important differences across countries regarding company law, contract law and fiscal matters will remain, and will facilitate the segmentation of markets. Given the high degree of integration already achieved, additional steps may require a higher degree of harmonization. As recently argued by Don Cruickshank (2003), chairman of the London Stock Exchange, if the member states of the EU really wish to achieve a fully integrated financial market, the EU institutions need a stronger political mandate. After all, more integration will imply that EU-wide objectives take precedence over local preferences, and this is not possible without further political integration. In the meantime, the current system, complemented by the use of the wide powers of the European Commission in competition policy to guarantee no discrimination, is probably the most that can be achieved.

References

Adam, K., T. Jappelli, A. Menichini, M. Padula and M. Pagano (2002), 'Analyse, compare and apply alternative indicators and monitoring methodologies to measure the evolution of capital market integration in the EU', Report to the European Commission, University of Salerno (January).

Bresnahan, Tim (1989), 'Empirical studies of industries with market power', in R. Schmalensee and R. D. Willig (eds.), *Handbook of Industrial Organization*, vol. II, Amsterdam: North Holland, pp. 1011–1058.

Buch, C. M. and R. P. Heinrich (2002), 'Financial integration in Europe and banking sector performance', in Heinemann and Jopp, 2002.

Corvoisier, S. and R. Gropp (2001), 'Bank concentration and retail interest rates', ECB Working Paper No. 72 (July), Frankfurt am Main: European Central Bank.

Cruickshank, Don (2003), 'A single market requires political union', *Financial Times*, 22 January.

Danthine, J. P., F. Giavazzi and E. L. von Thadden (2000), 'European financial markets after EMU: a first assessment', CEPR Discussion Paper 2413 (April), London: Centre for Economic Policy Research.

Danthine, J. P., F. Giavazzi, X. Vives and E. L. von Thadden (1999), 'The future of European banking', *Monitoring European Integration* No. 9, London: Centre for Economic Policy Research.

De Bondt, Gabe (2002), 'Retail bank interest pass-through: new evidence at the euro area level', ECB Working Paper No. 136 (April), Frankfurt am Main: European Central Bank.

Demirgüç-Kunt, A. and R. Levine (eds.) (2001), *Financial structure and economic growth: a cross-country comparison of banks, markets, and development*, Cambridge, MA: MIT Press.

Dermine, Jean (2002), 'European banking: past, present and future', Paper presented at 2nd ECB Central Banking Conference on 'The transformation of the European financial system', Frankfurt am Main, 24–25 October.

DeYoung, Robert (1999), 'Mergers and the changing landscape of commercial banking (part I)', *Chicago Fed Letter*, 145 (September): 1–3.

ECB [European Central Bank] (1999a), 'The effects of technology on the EU banking systems' (July), Frankfurt am Main: European Central Bank.

(1999b), 'Possible effects of EMU on the EU banking systems in the medium to long term' (February), Frankfurt am Main: European Central Bank.

(2000a), 'ECB mergers and acquisitions involving the EU banking industry – facts and implications' (December), Frankfurt am Main: European Central Bank.

(2000b), 'EU banks' margins and credit standards' (December), Frankfurt am Main: European Central Bank.

(2002a), 'Payment and securities settlement systems in the EU: addendum incorporating 2000 figures, blue book' (July), Frankfurt am Main: European Central Bank.

(2002b), 'Structural analysis of the EU banking sector, year 2001' (November), Frankfurt am Main: European Central Bank.

Economic Research Europe (1996), 'A study of the effectiveness and impact of internal market integration on the banking and credit sector', Report for the European Commission, Single Market Review, Brussels.

European Commission (2001), 'Financial market integration in the EU', *European Economy*, 73: 125–174.

(2002), 'Report by the economic and financial committee (EFC) on EU financial integration', Economic Papers No. 171, May, Brussels: Directorate General for Economic and Financial Affairs.

Giannetti, M., L. Guiso, T. Jappelli, M. Padula and M. Pagano (2002), 'Financial market integration, corporate financing and economic growth', Economic Papers No. 179, Final Report (22 November), Brussels: Directorate General for Economic and Financial Affairs.

Group of Ten (2001), 'Report on consolidation in the financial sector', January, available at www.bis.org.

Gual, J. (1993), 'La competencia en el mercado español de depósitos bancarios', *Moneda y Crédito* 196: 143–179.

(1999), 'Deregulation, integration and market structure in European banking', *Journal of the Japanese and International Economies*, 13 (4) (December): 372–396.

Gual, J. and D. Neven (1993), 'Deregulation of the European banking industry', *European Economy/Social Europe*, 3: 153–183.

Heinemann, F. and M. Jopp (2002), 'The benefits of a working European retail market for financial services', Report to the European Financial Services Round Table available at http://www.zew.de/en/forschung/erfstudyresults.html.

Humphrey, D. (1987), 'Cost dispersion and the measurement of economies in banking', *Federal Reserve Bank of Richmond Economics Review*, 73 (3) (May/June): 24–38.

Klemperer, Paul (1987), 'Markets with consumer switching costs', *Quarterly Journal of Economics*, 102 (2): 375–394.

London Economics (2002), 'Quantification of the macroeconomic impact of integration of EU financial markets', Report to the European Commission (November), Brussels.

Mojon, B. (2000), 'Financial structure and the interest rate channel of ECB monetary policy', ECB Working Paper No. 40 (November), Frankfurt am Main: European Central Bank.

Neven, Damien J. and Lars-Hendrik Röller (1999), 'An aggregate structural model of competition in the European banking industry', *International Journal of Industrial Organization*, 17 (7): 1059–1074.

Nevo, Aviv (2000), 'A practitioner's guide to estimation of random coefficients logit models of demand', *Journal of Economics and Management Strategy*, 9 (4) (Winter): 513–548.

Rosengreen, Eric (2002), 'Comment on European banking: past, present and future', Paper presented at 2nd ECB Central Banking Conference on 'The transformation of the European financial system', Frankfurt am Main, 24–25 October.

Schmalensee, R. (1989), 'Inter-industry studies of structure and performance', in R. Schmalensee and R. D. Willig (eds.), *Handbook of Industrial Organization*, vol. II, Amsterdam: North Holland, pp. 952–1009.

Schüler, M. and F. Heinemann (2002), 'How integrated are European retail financial markets? A cointegration analysis', in Heinemann and Jopp 2002.

Sun, J.-M. and J. Pelkmans (1995), 'Regulatory competition in the single market', *Journal of Common Market Studies*, 33 (1) (March): 67–89.

Van Empel, M. and A. Mörner (2000), 'Financial services and regional integration', in S. Claessens and M. Jansen (eds.), *The internationalization of financial services: issues and lessons for developing countries*, London: Kluwer, pp. 37–61.

White, L. (1996), 'Competition versus harmonization: an overview of international regulation of financial services', in C. Barfield (ed.), *International financial markets: harmonization versus competition*, Washington, DC: American Enterprise Institute, pp. 5–48.

Index

Spain (*cont.*)
  inflation, 114–115
  transition to democracy, 10
Stahl, K., 96
state aids, 122
stress, 53
subsidiarity, 12, 14
Sweden
  absenteeism, 53, 55
  child care, 44
  education, 45
  gas industry, 86
  parental leave, 43
  pensions, 60
  sick children, 43
  sickness benefits, 55

Tabellini, Guido, 8, 21, 24
taxation
  banking, 134
  behavioural adjustments, 40
  and budget deficits, 119–120
  EU differentials, 65
  fiscal policy and monetary policy,
    102–108
  household services, 54
  multiplicity of fiscal authorities,
    107–108
  unhealthy products, 56
telecommunications, 71, 76–80
temporary employees, 53
trade commissioner, 31
transparency
  banking, 130
  ECB inflation targeting, 105
  European Council, 12, 13
  national budgets, 122

UCITS, 134, 136, 138, 152
unemployment, 46–52
unemployment cultures, 51, 54
United Kingdom, *see* Britain
United States
  antitrust law, 94, 142
  banking, 140, 142–143, 150, 154
  budget deficit, 117
  Californian electricity crisis, 83, 89,
    93, 96–97

child care, 44
Constitution, 26
education, 45, 46
electoral college, 32
employment, 64
energy markets, 92–94
Glass–Steagall Act, 129
health insurance, 56
monetary policy, 106
political regime, 20, 37
pork barrel politics, 27
telecommunications, 78
utilities, *see* network utilities

values, common European, 11
Verhofstadt, Prime Minister Guy, 15
Virgin, 81
voucher systems, 45–46, 57, 63

water industry, 81
Weibull, J. W., 54
welfare benefits
  children, 42–46
  differences, 41
  dynamics, 39
  expenditure, 39
  financial viability, 40
  insider–outsider divide, 51
  issues, 39–42
  moral hazard, 40–41, 43, 52–53, 55,
    64
  old age, 58–63
  race to the bottom, 64–65
  and social changes, 41
  standardization, 66
  strength, 29, 39
  transferability, 65–66
  undesirable behavioural adjustments,
    40–41, 64
  unemployment, 46–52
Wikström, S., 57
Wolak, F. A., 93, 96
Wolfers, J. , 47
Wolff, Holger, 109
women, employment, 44, 53–54, 64
Wyplosz, Charles, 7

Yugoslavia crisis, 11